"*Make Work Matter* is a book that, like your work, matters. I have been working, teaching, and advocating for a deeper and broader integration of faith and work in hopes of a fuller realization of God's invitation to participate in the ongoing incarnation through our work for over four decades. Happily, Michaela O'Donnell of Fuller Seminary's De Pree Center is one of my favorite and most trusted colleagues in this mission. Michaela is a practitioner and a doer—as am I. She's not your typical academic or "thought leader." She's built businesses, careers, and a life. She just happens to be attentive enough to what has and hasn't been helpful in her practice to have also become a brilliant teacher and communicator. This book goes the next step beyond the many books now espousing good ideas about the sacred value of good work and moves into how to actively discern, find, and do it. The pursuit of good work takes work—and this book is a powerful tool to focus your labors and ease the challenge of that worthy pursuit. I recommend it heartily."

**Dave Evans**, cofounder, Stanford Life Design Lab; coauthor, *Designing Your Life* and *Designing Your Work Life*; and venture partner, Praxis Labs

"Most of us spend more waking hours on work than anything else. In the midst of the demands of navigating the twists and turns of work today, *Make Work Matter* gives you the road map you need to maximize those hours for your own growth, calling, fulfillment, and formation."

**Kara Powell**, PhD, chief of leadership formation and executive director, Fuller Youth Institute; coauthor, *3 Big Questions That Change Every Teenager*

D1622322

"Dr. Michaela O'Donnell's *Make Work Matter* offers a life-giving, meaning-making invitation, recipe, and coaching session about work—all in one. She is a very motivating exemplar of what she writes about, and her voice resonates with lived wisdom, creativity, and courage. In a time of extraordinary changes in work, turn here for true help."

**Mark Labberton**, president, Fuller Theological Seminary

"Honestly, there aren't many people who can actually help you make your work matter. A challenge like that requires a blend of theory, theology, and pragmatism. Most people have expertise in just one, so too often their advice is (at best) half baked. Michaela is different. She's an entrepreneur, practical theologian, and academic. She gets the messiness of it all and teaches us to wrestle with the possibilities. This book, like Michaela, is approachable, down to earth, and just plain helpful. Michaela, where were you when I was trying to find meaning in the junkyard?"

**Roy Goble**, CEO of Goble Properties; cofounder, PathLight International; author, *Junkyard Wisdom: Resisting the Whisper of Wealth in a World of Broken Parts* and *Salvaged: Leadership Lessons Pulled from the Junkyard*

"This is one of those books that ends up dog-eared, coffee-stained, and filled with scribbles in the margins. In the whitewater of a rapidly changing world of work, Michaela O'Donnell is the trusted guide you are looking for. She'll be the first to tell you that navigating issues of work, career, vocation, identity, resilience, failure, and—yes—purpose, meaning, and success is not easy. Indeed, you are likely going to find yourself falling in and gasping for air. But this book is part lifeline, part instruction manual, part map and compass, and a whole lot of hard-earned wisdom. At every fork in the river of your career, you will come back to it again and again."

**Tod Bolsinger**, author, *Tempered Resilience: How Leaders Are Formed in the Crucible of Change*

"As a fellow laborer in the faith and work space with Michaela, I wanted to cheer out loud when I read her book, because it is such practical wisdom for the angst around 'call' for many workers, but especially Millennials. Her work reflects not only theological truth, but also the hard-earned wisdom that only one who has walked the path can unpack. Unsure of your work's role in God's redemptive story? Feeling the urge to pontificate your vocation but without a theological rudder? Look no further. Michaela's book has come to lead you into a journey of understanding your work with God at the center."

**Missy Wallace**, managing director, Global Strategic Services; Faith Work Content Specialist, Redeemer City to City

"*Make Work Matter* is surprising in many ways. Unlike so many other books on work, it is based, not just on the writer's solid convictions, but also on research into the working lives of real people. Yet the book is also filled with astute theological insights that are presented as if from a good friend seeking wisdom rather than from an esteemed professor with all the answers. Michaela generously opens up her own life to us, inviting us into a shared process of discovery and vocational discernment. *Make Work Matter* is perfect for folks in the early stages of figuring out their work lives. But, unexpectedly, it also speaks powerfully to older readers who are wondering about God's callings in the third third of life."

**Mark D. Roberts**, PhD, author, *Life for Leaders* and *52 Workday Prayers*; founder, De Pree Center's Flourishing in the Third Third of Life Initiative

"We learn best through story and metaphor. Through these genres, this much-needed field guide helps us to make sense and meaning out of our daily work, how it connects with our calling (an oft-used but little-understood term), and where that fits with our identity as Christians. Theologically grounded and eminently practical, this guide is both a relief and a gift. A relief, in that it untangles and creates pathways with real tools toward clarifying and uncovering calling. A gift, in that Michaela shares her own journey and story with all its highs and lows, generously and vulnerably, to illuminate the way for those who follow behind. An intrepid journey not for the faint of heart, now one has a faithful and experienced travel partner with a backpack full of tools, insight and wisdom."

**Lisa Slayton**, founder and CEO, Tamim Partners; director, CityGate, an initiative of Denver Institute for Faith and Work

"In *Make Work Matter*, Michaela O'Donnell helps us understand the delicate intersection of our work and our calling. Through interviews of others who have already navigated the journey and her own personal experience, she helps us understand that the question is not what we are going to do, but rather who we are going to become. If you are trying to find a purpose for life and work that has meaning, *Make Work Matter* is a great place to start!"

**Dee Ann Turner**, vice president, Chick-fil-A, Inc. (retired);
author, *Bet on Talent* and *Crush Your Career*

"Michaela O'Donnell is the rare combination of an academic-practitioner who provides useful step-by-step guidance for how to create meaning and purpose in one's daily work, and she does so in a style that is a genuine joy to read. Using stories from real life, O'Donnell shows that the entrepreneurial way is not only for those who start big companies but for anyone who is navigating the ever-changing world of work. *Make Work Matter* is a gift for those at the beginning of their careers, for those whose jobs are changing, for the entrepreneur starting a new venture, and for anyone asking questions about how their faith and their work can illuminate one another."

**Denise Daniels**, PhD, Hudson T. Harrison Professor
of Entrepreneurship, Wheaton College

"Michaela has lived the words on these pages and writes as if she is in the room speaking right to you. If you feel stuck with no clear path forward or you want to feel liberated to be creative and take risks in this new world of work, this book is your guide. If you are eager to make your work matter and to navigate the new work landscape with new tools and clarity of vision, Michaela's book will be a comfort and an inspiration. Michaela will meet you in what she describes as your 'holy wrestling,' and you will finish this book more confident, more capable, and more courageous."

**Angela Gorrell**, PhD, assistant professor of practical theology, Baylor University; author, *The Gravity of Joy: A Story of Being Lost and Found*

"With the compassion of a doting shepherd, the precision of a practical theologian, and the discerning eye of a cultural exegete, Dr. Michaela O'Donnell has gifted us with a down-to-earth book written for twenty-five-to-forty-five-year-old working Christians who find themselves smack dab in the midst of a new work world saddled with old tools and sadly ill equipped to be a world changer. Through masterful and compelling storytelling and end-of-chapter practical exercises, O'Donnell provides this age-group a blueprint for their own maturation for the path forward."

**Luke Brad Bobo**, director of strategic partnerships, Made to Flourish, Overland Park, KS

# *Make*
# *Work*
# *Matter*

# *Make Work Matter*

## YOUR GUIDE TO MEANINGFUL WORK IN A CHANGING WORLD

### MICHAELA O'DONNELL, PHD

BakerBooks
a division of Baker Publishing Group
Grand Rapids, Michigan

Published by Baker Books
a division of Baker Publishing Group
PO Box 6287, Grand Rapids, MI 49516-6287
www.bakerbooks.com

Printed in the United States of America

Library of Congress Cataloging-in-Publication Data
Names: O'Donnell, Michaela, 1983– author.
Title: Make work matter : your guide to meaningful work in a changing world / Michaela O'Donnell, Ph.D.
Description: Grand Rapids, MI : Baker Books, a division of Baker Publishing Group, [2021] | Includes bibliographical references.
Identifiers: LCCN 2021006696 | ISBN 9781540901606 (paperback) | ISBN 9781540901958 (casebound) | ISBN 9781493432363 (ebook)
Subjects: LCSH: Work—Religious aspects. | Vocational guidance. |Self-actualization (Psychology)
Classification: LCC BJ1498 .O34 2021 | DDC 174—dc23
LC record available at https://lccn.loc.gov/2021006696

The author is represented by WordServe Literary Group, www.wordserveliterary.com.

Baker Publishing Group publications use paper produced from sustainable forestry practices and post-consumer waste whenever possible.

21  22  23  24  25  26  27      7  6  5  4  3  2  1

To Dan—I am so grateful for our love.

# Contents

# PART ONE

# Where Do You Want to Go?

You can't really know where you are going until you know where you have been.

Maya Angelou

# 1

# Name Where You're Stuck

I met James on a crisp morning in the rec room of a dusty church. With sandy brown hair and a kind smile, he came up to introduce himself before we got started. I was there to teach a workshop on calling. He was there for the bagels.

As the workshop began and the sun started to heat our room, James transformed from a bright-eyed breakfast eater into what seemed like quite a grumpy guy. His arms were folded, and his brow was furrowed. He sat stoic for hours not saying a word. When the group talked about how we might trade the definitions of calling we'd been fed by society for a more biblical approach, James sunk lower into his chair. I really couldn't tell if he was pissed at me, at God, or at someone else. But now he was definitely angry.

Several hours into the workshop, he raised his hand. It was a small group, and the rest of us were well past the hand-raising niceties. But I was so surprised he wanted to talk that I halted midsentence and walked over to him, grabbing a chair on my way. I sat down so that we were eye to eye before I motioned for him to speak.

He opened up through what I can only describe as "rage tears" about all the unhelpful jargon he'd been fed by church leaders about "his calling." Through gritted teeth, he talked in bursts about the enormous debt he had incurred as a law student and how he was woefully unable to fulfill his own internal expectations of being the breadwinner for his family. When I prodded a little further about how folks had contributed to his unmet expectations, he sarcastically recited a mantra that he said was spoken over him time and time again: "If it's God's will, it'll be God's bill."

I gasped at the recklessness of who I can only assume were grown adults instilling this kind of blanketed hope in James. How dare they imply that if he sensed a call to a specific career path, God would make sure he didn't incur any financial burden! There he was, likely hundreds of thousands of dollars in debt and rightfully hurt, rightfully angry. After his tears dried, he reassumed his posture—arms crossed and brow furrowed. As hard as it was for me to just let him be, I did. Afterward, I tiptoed toward each word I spoke lest I be added to the list of unhelpful leaders with unhelpful mantras and do further damage to his heart.

A few days later, I got an unexpected email from James. His note wasn't long, but I'll never forget it. He wrote to tell me how our time together had helped him get unstuck about an idea he'd been working on for years. It had helped him unlock things about his work that he didn't even know were locked up.

Only then was I able to realize that I had witnessed something beyond anger. I had witnessed *holy wrestling*—the honest and ongoing inner tussle about whatever it is God is up to in and around us. I am convinced that his honest wrestling helped him reckon with the forces from his past that had caused him pain. And that this was key to whatever creative breakthrough he had. I'm convinced because I've seen time and time again how listening to our pain, naming where we're stuck, and doing a good bit of wrestling can set the stage for a deep and transformative journey.

My own holy wrestling started in a surprising place. As I sat crisscrossed on a wooden floor, I thumped the keys of a grey typewriter I had purchased online. My task? To enter people's personal information, box by box, into forms for the state of California. Every time my mind wandered (which was often), I thumped the wrong key. This meant I had to lift the little bar that holds the paper down, pull the form out, cover my mistake in white-out, and try again. Filling in these tedious forms was my first job out of grad school.

I'd recently spent three long, tiring years—and borrowed $60,000—to get a master's degree. Like most of my classmates, I hoped my degree in theology would launch me into work that would "change the world" or at least feel purposeful and fulfilling. Yet there I was, doing mind-numbing data entry and about as far from changing the world as I could be. There I was, longing for more in a way that I couldn't quite name.

To complicate things further, I was newly married. Dan and I met in grad school, so lucky us—we had a pair of newly minted (and expensive) degrees that, as it turns out, weren't very marketable in a recession. As I hit dead end after dead end with organizations I admired, I started to feel really discouraged. I was following all the career advice I'd heard along the way but still coming up short every time. It didn't take long before all my hustling gave way to said discouragement and then anxiety. And with looming bills, it felt impossible to allow myself the space my soul needed to grieve my unfulfilled expectations. So I just kept hustling.

Fairly quickly, Dan and I realized that if we wanted to love our work, it would be up to us to figure something else out—to improvise as we went. I wondered, *What sort of work should we pursue? Were we dreaming when we hoped that we could get paid and utilize our degrees at the same time? What was God really calling us to do?*

The truth I was too afraid to admit was this: I was educated but unprepared. I'd been sent into a new world of work with old tools. I felt stuck and alone—with no idea of what was next. And I didn't quite have the frameworks to understand that my work—even the most mundane parts of it—already mattered to God. *Was I asking for too much to hope for meaningful work that I loved?* In other words, I was wrestling.

When I think of wrestling, I can't help but think of Jacob— grandson of Abraham, son of Isaac and Rebekah, brother of Esau. Jacob has always felt to me like such a beautifully complex person. On the one hand, God calls him to a life of leadership before he's even born. On the other hand, Jacob lives a life of conflict, especially with his brother. In a way, Jacob's entire story seems to be marked by wrestling, a theme that comes into focus when he literally wrestles a stranger in the middle of the night (Gen. 32:22–31). He's on the way to a potentially contentious meeting with his brother when out of fear he sends his fellow travelers on ahead. Then, when it's just Jacob and the dark night sky, we're told that he wrestles with an unknown figure all night long (there are many theories on who that stranger might be!).

Just before daylight, Jacob seems to have the upper hand on the stranger and literally demands a blessing in order to let his sparring partner free (again, Jacob is a beautifully complicated human being). But the stranger does not bless him—at least not in the way Jacob might have been hoping for. Instead, the stranger gives Jacob a *new name.* No longer will he be called Jacob, which means "trickster." His new name is Israel, which means "God rules or preserves."[1] God's presence in the holy wrestling transforms Jacob's identity and quite literally how he walks through the world. His assurance on the way forward is that God is with him.

We too can trust that holy wrestling will change us. It might change how we perceive ourselves or God or how we walk through the world. Whether our holy wrestling happens in the dark, through rage tears, or in the mundane thumping of typewriter keys, underneath every moment of wrestling is an invitation for some kind of transformation.

Perhaps you too are wrestling. Maybe you're like I was, and you're having a hard time finding work you love. Or maybe you're like James, and you've got so much debt that doing work you love feels like just one more luxury you can't afford.

Maybe you've wanted to change careers, but you're afraid that you're too old and that you'll be too far behind. Maybe you never imagined yourself getting a traditional job, but you feel overwhelmed because there aren't enough models or mentors for what you want to do. Maybe you have lots of creative ideas but don't know how they go together or where to start.

Maybe you're trying to balance kids and a career. But because there's too much to do and too much to pay for, you wind up feeling guilty about everything. Maybe you're tired and overwhelmed, and you just need a break.

Maybe it's not so much that something is wrong in your work but that you're exhausted by the relentless pace of change in the world. Your heart and mind are jostled by how fast the world is moving and how all that change creates new demands for you and your work.

As part of your wrestling, maybe you're also holding on to hope—believing that God is near and trustworthy and that you too are named and called and welcomed into the work of God in this world.

## New World, Old Tools

We don't make our way to the meaningful work we crave without a bit of holy wrestling. We need to outfit ourselves with the tools to do this deep work. Because change is happening so fast, most of us are perpetually living and working in a new world with old tools. This requires us to both reevaluate old tools that have worked well for generations and invest in new tools suited for navigating change. In order to build a new toolkit, we have to start with naming why the old one no longer works. The last thing we want to do is replace outdated tools with unhelpful ones.

Start by thinking about why there are fewer places where people can count on steady and long-term work. Consider that even as recently as a generation ago, it was common for people to stay with a company or in an industry for the duration of their careers. Young farmers became old farmers. Junior executives became senior ones. Teachers sometimes stayed with schools for thirty years. But today, the average person changes jobs many times.[2] And the number of people active in the independent economy has more than tripled in the last two decades.[3] Why is it that over forty million people have some kind of side hustle, do gig work, or are working for themselves full-time?

Picture a set of well-worn paths that are eroding or perhaps even barricaded. The disappearing of seemingly well-worn paths has a lot to do with the fact that our collective relationship to knowledge has changed. Hear me out. As a society, we've moved from the Industrial Age to the Information Age. If the Industrial Age was a time marked by efficiency and mass production because of machines, the Information Age is a time marked by cultural disruption and digital acceleration powered by technology.

Knowledge is easier to both access and distribute than it was just a couple decades ago. Take something as simple as a recipe for banana bread. Thirty years ago, if you wanted to make banana bread for the first time, chances are you would have consulted a family member or a cookbook you owned. The information you could access came via established and predictable channels.

If you set out to make banana bread today, you have the option to consult not only family or a trusty cookbook but also the entire world. If you google "banana bread recipe," you are met with over 400 million relevant hits in less than a second. And because of the power of algorithms, the first several hundred hits are recipes you might actually want to try. Let's say that after reading a dozen recipes, you decide to bake a hybrid—essentially creating your own new recipe. Later, you take a picture of your creation and post it along with the recipe on social media using #bananabread. Now any number of people you've never met have access to your knowledge and can make the bread you invented.

As our ways of knowing have diversified, how we conceptualize and access work has been disrupted. Instead of a fixed set of well-worn career paths, we now have seemingly limitless opportunities. Some of the same jobs remain, but the paths toward them feel different. Plus, there are so many new ways to make a living than there were just a decade ago. As with making banana bread, it is now up to individuals to piece together something that works for them.

Beyond just how we access work, diversified knowledge streams have impacted how we do our work, what we work on, and who we work with. Consider the apps or platforms you use that weren't invented ten years ago. Consider the projects you've worked on in the last year and all the different skills you had to have to do so. And consider how an increasingly diverse workforce changes everything. From an aging population to transnational companies to the shifting ethnic demographics of the population of America, chances are that you're working in less homogeneous groups than the workers of thirty years ago. These shifts make work more complex (and more wonderful and more like the kingdom of God!). A more diverse workforce makes the inequities that are still so deeply ingrained in our society feel both increasingly more noticeable and less tolerable in our workplaces. As a result, some companies are rightly reckoning with racial and gender equity in their ranks and practices. Interestingly, that reckoning is often not coming from the center of an organization. In other words, it's not happening on a well-worn path. No, the reckoning is coming largely through decentralized yet interconnected, well-organized individuals on the margins. Knowledge feels flipped inside out.

At the heart of all this disruption is a shift in what I'll call the *burden of responsibility*. When knowledge is centralized, the implicit burden of responsibility for making sure the world and the economy work is largely on the places that presumed to hold that knowledge—educational institutions, government, big systems, and corporations. The results were well-worn pathways in and out of those centers and guides who knew the way. But as our relationship with knowledge has changed and when knowledge feels flipped inside out, we're forced to wrestle with what was once assumed. When this happens, sometimes the center grasps for power and life and fights back against the new ways of doing things. Other times, the center fractures and disintegrates. Still other times, there's a blending of the old and the new. Whatever the case, we are—in real time—synthesizing knowledge from a variety of sources so that we can go where no path yet exists! If you ever feel as if you're just sort of making it up as you go, know that you're not alone. We're all in this shift together.

It's not only information that's more accessible. It's people too. Technology has made our greatest resource as a species—ourselves—feel constantly available. As a result, we live in an *always-on, on-demand* culture. Think about what this means for expectations and boundaries between work and the rest of our lives. They start to get blurry fast, especially if a portion of our work happens on a computer or via email—the same places from which we send texts to our friends or look at pictures of our families. Thirty years ago, if someone worked in an office environment, they were largely out of reach after hours. A nine-to-five job was just that. But today, when the average person checks their smartphone a hundred times a day, it's harder to distinguish if and when we're truly unplugged.

It's no surprise, then, that our always-on, on-demand way of being has given birth to *hustle culture*. As a culture, we reward accomplishments and ambition. That's not all bad, of course. In fact, hustle can be an agent of good. But when the collective speak is that every goal we meet was worth whatever it took to get there, things get problematic. It's painful for me to admit how often I've found myself buying into hyped-up hustle as a viable path forward, how often I've abused my own energy in the name of accomplishments, progress, and meaningful work.

Now consider the way the West prepares its citizens for work and if the tools we need today are prioritized in our spaces for formal learning: Do we prioritize preparing people for continuous change and ambiguity? Do we work to cultivate resilience and creativity above all else in the classroom? Do we encourage experimentation with skills such as empathy and risk-taking as means for career exploration? Do we teach people to mitigate pressures to unhealthy hustle in an on-demand world?

As an educator myself, I can say that it's been nearly impossible to keep up with the rate of change in the world and to apply it fully to lessons in the classroom. Partly, this is because our educational systems are built around fixed milestones, reflecting the former era where pathways into work were clearer and more well established. Starting in kindergarten, young minds progress through different phases of education—elementary, middle, and high school, and eventually college. In every phase, there are clear goals that define the progression. The gifts of humans we call teachers are charged with helping students to reach these milestones of success. The measures we're all aiming for are set in place by schools and districts, government, and accreditation boards at various points. It's almost as if we're on an assembly line.

One of the central goals of this assembly line is to adequately prepare us for the workforce. The assumption of the well-worn path is that checking certain boxes sets us up to contribute meaningfully and productively to society. Up until fairly recently, this assembly line would pop out workers, ready to take their places in the industries of America—industries such as business, manufacturing, education, retail, health care, entertainment, and government.

But today, because the world is changing faster than education can keep up with, there's a gap between our education and preparation for work. Closing this gap is the work that now undergirds all the rest of our work. We won't solve all this at once or all by ourselves. Just when we adopt and adapt to this new world of work, it's bound to change again.

## The New World of Work Is, Well . . . a Lot

The primary characteristic of this new world of work is change. When we experience change, we experience loss.

27

When we experience loss, we should grieve. As I sat there on my living room floor, filling in forms on a typewriter, I had no playbook for the way forward. *What was I even doing with my life?* I was tired from all the fruitless hustling. I was burned out because I felt as if the system wasn't working for me. I was discouraged about the gap between where I was and where I wanted to be. And I felt paralyzed when I tried to imagine my next steps. I wonder if you too have experienced symptoms that reveal the new world of work is taking a toll on you, such as feeling overwhelmed, anxious, or lonely. These are, of course, just three. You might create your own list or build on this one as you go.

### *Symptom #1: You're Feeling Overwhelmed*

Working in an on-demand world is overwhelming. Lacking guides is overwhelming. Adapting to changing technologies, new expectations, and new relationships is overwhelming. Feeling like certainty is always just out of reach is overwhelming. Yet here we are, feeling like it's up to us to figure out our own way forward. And work is a big deal for us—partly because we need money to live and partly because it's been deemed a vehicle for our self-expression and significance. Turns out, that's a lot of pressure to put on our work—and on ourselves.[4]

The feeling of overwhelm can show up in different ways. In the groups and classes I lead, I ask people to put images to their feelings of overwhelm. One person described the chronic tension she carries in her jaw because of all of her work stress. Another described himself stuck in quicksand because he felt paralyzed about how to take steps toward his dreams. Still another person had us picture with him a deep hole in the earth—which represented the pit of self-doubt he feels when he's overwhelmed and depressed.

When I get overwhelmed, I feel overstimulated. The image I share with groups is that of a hamster on a wheel. When I'm operating out of my least healthy self, I respond to overstimulation by dialing up my hustle. This, as you might guess, is not actually a great antidote to feeling overwhelmed and in fact yields a lot more stuff I have to deal with.

Even though I know better, when life feels so full and each thing I'm doing feels valuable, I let the messages of hustle culture guide me. They tell me to power through—that I don't have the margin to slow down and that I don't have time to rest. I quite literally ignore the signals my body sends me about needing water and food and sleep. When this happens, I find myself working at two in the morning, skipping meals, and anxiously checking my phone all the time. Let me tell you, I have never once been proud of something I've produced when I've ignored the needs of my body. And my body has never once thanked me for powering through.

*How do you deal with feeling overwhelmed?* Do you get depressed and find it hard to keep going? Do you withdraw from others? Do you find some sort of an escape? Do you dial up your hustle? Do you set boundaries with your phone or work email? Do you spend time with people who are energizing? Do you care for yourself with a long walk or a day of rest? Again, if you're feeling overwhelmed by the changes in our world, know that you're not alone.

### Symptom #2: You're Feeling Anxious

In its most basic form, anxiety is fear about what might happen in the future. We can feel anxious for many reasons, including when we feel as though we don't have enough information about a situation. Remember Thomas, the disciple who just couldn't believe that Jesus had been resurrected until he had more information? Until he could poke the places where Jesus had been nailed to the cross (John 20:24–29)? Maybe Thomas was just anxious.

Anxiety isn't all bad. It can actually be a healthy human response to unknown circumstances, helping us notice threats and make decisions. But as the world is accelerating and becoming less and less predictable, it's too much for our brains to handle. When we're anxious about work and also about climate change or politics or stuff going on in our families, we become exponentially anxious—each anxiety-producing thought feeding off one another. Our brains and hearts are taking in more than they were meant to. And we must be on the lookout for how quickly healthy anxiety morphs into unproductive and debilitating fear, limiting our capacity to function and flourish.

In a world that demands so much from individuals, the message is that we are to be the heroes of our own stories, that we alone have to gather all the information. What's more, in the name of opportunity, we're even told that we can achieve anything we set our minds to—we can be anything we dream! Limitless possibilities and the responsibility to ensure they all come to fruition are an extraordinary amount of pressure for one person. Also, what this tragically means is that if everything goes wrong, there's no one but ourselves to blame.

We all have our own triggers for worry: money, relationships, happiness. One of the places I find myself getting anxious is something I affectionately call *the gap*. The gap is the space between where I am and where I want to be in my career. When Dan and I first started our creative agency, the gap felt all-consuming. In those early days, we worked out of our dining room. We lived on cheap takeout and boxed macaroni and cheese. We often worked until nine or ten at night, putting in the hard work it takes to build a business. As much as I loved that process of building our business, if I'm honest, part of what motivated my hard work was my anxiety about closing the gap.

My anxiety about the gap (and my lack of naming my feelings!) made it hard to enjoy what was going well. I'd hear of a client someone else landed and my first response would be to feel a hot pang of envy. Or I'd hear of a promotion a friend got, and I'd feel both happy and jealous that she was succeeding at a faster rate than I was. I was so focused on myself that I couldn't celebrate what God was doing in others.

As the world of work continues to change, there will be more unknowns. Part of your work is to be able to identify and name your anxiety. Consider when your heart rate goes up, the tension in your shoulders feels pronounced, or your stomach feels tight. Maybe you replay conversations that you're worried about. Or maybe you find yourself putting off a task because you're dreading an unknown outcome.[5] With so much going on, it's understandable that you're anxious.

### *Symptom #3: You're Feeling Lonely*

The "you're on your own" vibe that undergirds our new world is exhausting. It's unpredictable and chaotic. It's scary. And at times, it's lonely.

At the end of this chapter you will have an opportunity to name your own symptoms in the form of frustrations and then to consider what they reveal about what you're longing for. Let me tell you now that one of the most common frustrations—or pain points—I hear people name in some form or another is loneliness. People feel isolated in their work for various reasons: relational issues, remote work, economic instability, and inequitable systems.

I'd like to tease out inequitable systems a bit, mostly because I think it impacts nearly everything else. In America, it's probably no surprise that our systems are built to privilege some and alienate others. That doesn't mean that the people who benefit are bad people per se, but that the rules don't favor everyone equally. Even when as a society we feel as though we're past realities like racism and sexism and any other ism, issues surface that make it clear we've got a long way to go. Yet as we shift into an era marked by the democratization of knowledge, rise in independent work, and diversification of our workforce, inequitable systems feel not only all the more inequitable but also as if maybe their days are increasingly limited.

When I graduated with my doctorate, I did so alongside eight men. As part of the ceremony, each person stood up and gave a short speech. Nearly every man expressed heartfelt gratitude through tears to his family for the time they sacrificed being with him while he completed the doctoral process.

When it was my turn to speak, I turned my shoulders so that I was looking straight at my then two-year-old daughter. As I gently said her name, she stopped playing with the doll in her hand. I spoke to her as if we were the only two in the room. Through my own mounting tears, I whispered, "Evelyn, someday I will tell you the story of how I wrote a dissertation while you slept." Though I hadn't planned to make a point about patriarchy and how it played a role in the obvious gender imbalance on stage that day, that is what ended up happening.

Why did my story sound so different from my colleagues? Because whenever possible, I chose not to sacrifice time with my kid but instead my own sleep—my own well-being. I did so not because I am an especially self-sacrificial person but because I was playing by the rules of patriarchy. In a patriarchal system, one of the central ways we make sense of male identity (and therefore assess the value of a man) is in relation to their role as workers. If a man has a good job (or in the new world of work, good *jobs*!) and provides financially for a family (if he has one), society thinks positively of that man. One way that as a society we express value for male identity through work is that we deem it acceptable for families to make sacrifices for Dad's work.

On the flip side, one of the primary ways patriarchy assesses a woman's value is in relation to her role as a wife and mother. The underlying message so many women get is that it's great if we work as long as it doesn't interfere with our other roles too much. This is why I probably missed out on hundreds of hours of sleep. And don't get me wrong, I love my kid (now kids). But if I'm honest, part of the reason I sacrificed my sleep instead of my time with her was guilt. Guilt that I wasn't being the mom she needed, and guilt that I wasn't a superpowered mom who could play by the rules of patriarchy and break them at the same time. Goodness, did that make me feel lonely.

Many of us are lonely and believe we have to hide it. We're physically drained and literally tired, like I was, but we're also guilt-ridden, worried, and potentially despairing without any companions to share with or help. We're wondering what and who we can trust in this unpredictable world.

Overwhelmed. Anxious. Lonely. It's a lot.

Whatever our symptoms are, left untended they can affect our health, our relationships, and our emotional well-being. This is what happened to my friend Sarah. Sarah is one of the most talented graphic designers I know. She has a thriving studio where she prides herself on subverting the hustle and embracing a slower pace. But this wasn't always the case. Her journey to get there was a traumatic one. I've heard her tell the story of her tipping point many times.

Years ago, Sarah crouched hidden under her office desk on the fifth floor of a downtown skyscraper. It was the third night in a month she'd had to sleep at work to meet a project deadline. Life as a junior architect was not unfolding as she had imagined. Fresh out of school, she dreamed of making cities beautiful. Instead, she found herself working insane hours on projects such as shopping malls and parking structures and under immense pressure to hustle. That particular morning, she found herself on the floor because she felt stuck; she wanted out but didn't have any idea what she'd do next.

After her third wave of tears had passed, she crawled out from under her desk and made a beeline to her boss's office. She quit in bursts, partly apologizing and partly trying to find words to convey just how much pressure she was under. It had become too much. The rules of success in that system just didn't work for her.

As she was explaining things to her boss, she had the growing sense that she was leaving not only her job at the firm but also her career as an architect. Yet she had been so sure that God had called her to this work. She walked out partly relieved and partly anxious—totally burned out but also certain that whatever she did next needed to not make her feel so horrible.

If we don't name the symptoms—and their root causes— that reveal the new world of work is taking a toll on us, it'll cost us things we can't afford to give. It'll cost us our health. It'll hurt our relationships. And we'll have a hard time making our way toward the work that God indeed calls us to do.

## Build a New Toolkit

Even in the midst of so much overwhelm, many of us remain curious. Hopeful. Expectant. We sense deep down that God is calling us to lives of meaning and purpose. So we need tools that help us seek God in the wrestling, navigate change, discern next steps, and at the same time earn a paycheck to pay for life.

After enough time sitting on the floor filling in those forms, my husband and I started our own branding and video company. A few years into that work, I found myself curious to know more about people who had figured out how to achieve success in the midst of a changing world. I was still running my business but also working on my PhD. The time had come for me to name what I was going to study, and it was these questions about work and calling that I gravitated toward.

I took my research findings and paired them with theological reflection to come up with a set of tools that people can use in order to discover more about themselves, God's callings, and their work. But it wasn't enough to have a theoretical method for how this might work. So I've spent the years since finishing my degree testing the tools with hundreds of people in lab-like classrooms, workshops, retreats, small groups, and coaching sessions. Like any process, testing helped me iterate the tools—removing what wasn't helpful and clarifying what was.

Whether you're hoping to move from stuck to unstuck, be liberated to take new risks, or discover deeper truths about what God has for you, I trust that there's something in this book and in these tools for you. We're all on a journey, through which we are indeed invited to join God in changing the world and along the way be changed ourselves.

Think of this book like a map. As you read it, you'll *do the work you need to do* and lay aside the rest. My hope is that the stories, data, and theological frameworks will help you to do the following:

1. Define where you are in this season of work
2. Embrace what the Bible says (and doesn't say) about calling
3. Develop a mindset and habits suited for a new world of work
4. Reflect on and work out ways that sustain you for the journey

You're here—in this book and in this season of your life—to do the work you need to do. I wholeheartedly believe that many of our paths toward meaningful work start with our honest reflection with both God and ourselves. While we might want quick fixes or step-by-step solutions, wrestling is rarely prescriptive. My hope is that you'll consider trading a life powered by hustle or filled with anxiety for one with healthy rhythms of reflection and rest. That you'll be able to embrace your own limits as you lean into praising a limitless God. And that you'll trust that you are indeed named and called and welcomed into the work of God in the world.

> EXERCISE: **Name Where You're Stuck**

Journal or reflect on the following questions:

1. Consider your pain points in work. Where do you feel frustrated, disappointed, or overwhelmed?
2. What do these reveal about what you're wrestling with?
3. What does what you're wrestling with reveal about what you're longing for?

## 2

# Lean In and Let Go

I've learned to slow down when I talk about the changing world of work. In a workshop, from a stage, or around a meeting table, I take in a long breath and then let my words fill the room. I deliver the news that we already know: "Work is dramatically different than it was just a generation ago." In fact, for many, work is dramatically different than it was just a few years ago.

I am met with a chorus of exhales, small groans, and head nods that I've learned over time reveal that we feel change deep in our bones. Sometimes we feel change as a seemingly constant need to learn new skills or adapt to new structures at work. Other times we're worried about money as we cobble together gigs or lack the safety net of a pension. Plus, amid whatever is happening in our work, we're trying to make sense of how what's happening globally impacts what we do personally—whether it's the fight for racial equity, a global pandemic, or climate change. We wonder what implications these tectonic shifts have on our individual place in the world. We wonder how to move beyond experiencing the weight of change and move toward being part of the change the world needs.

As I listen to people talk about their experiences, I hear layers of exhaustion, worry, confusion, and heartache. People are grieving. People are quick to name that the rules of work that governed the generations before us no longer hold up today. We're grieving security and certainty, a pension and a plan. We're grieving not having the necessary skills or having too much debt, or we're doubting if we really can figure out how to integrate who we feel like we are with what we do for work.

But when I talk with these same people, I also hear hope and joy and creativity. I hear stories about complex problems people are trying to solve or the ways they're seeing God at work in their communities and their families. Many of these folks have truly innovative ideas for how to make a difference through their work. All of this is why I've come to believe that the changing world of work is part grief and part hope: grief for what was, hope for what might be; grief for what felt doable, hope for what feels possible.

Amid all this, what I hear most commonly is people's desire to discern how to move forward. How do we keep pace with a God who is on the move? How do we join God in work that matters?

Understanding how God is moving and discerning our place in it requires us to name where we currently are. In chapter 1, I framed much of the naming where we are as internal work—honestly reflecting on and naming where we're stuck and what it is we long for. Now we turn to the task of naming where we are collectively so that we might ask, *How does what's happening to all of us impact each of us?*

At the heart of our collective reality is the fact that change is accelerating. As the world is speeding up, it feels as if there's an almost subversive invitation to get really, really clear about what matters and to forget the rest—to tune in to what matters and let that drown out the noise. As part of this invitation, there's what feels like a healthy pressure to develop competencies and tools that generations before us have not needed to prioritize in quite the same way. Today, we've got to focus on cultivating skills such as grief, resilience, adaptability, agility, creativity, emotional intelligence, empathy, self-reflection, and the ability to perform well amid ambiguity. We'll address each of these in different ways, but for now, know that all the skills we need have one thing in common: they're what help people navigate change.

## Welcome to the Age of Overwhelm!

We feel widespread change on a personal, everyday level. We carry it as stress in our shoulders or bags under our eyes. It comes to the surface in the way we snap at our kids or neglect texts from our friends. Change is a force that requires attention. Our bodies and our minds require space to process and cope with all that's happening. It takes zooming out and talking with others to trace the patterns of what's happening in our society and in our individual lives. It takes time to unravel how all this impacts our everyday experiences.

I want to zoom out and talk about four big unspoken rules that informally govern our new world of work. Each unspoken rule has to do with a change in how work used to be versus how it is today. I'll affectionately call these the *Big Unspokens*:

1. *Grab a paddle because we've traded static career paths for dynamic ones.* In the past, a person's career journey was a lot like riding up an escalator. Now it's much more like kayaking down white water rapids.

2. *Prepare to be unprepared because change is our new constant companion.* Previously, education, technical skills, and good networks were enough to set someone on the path to success. Now, in addition to these things, people need the ability to thrive in the midst of constant change.

3. *Navigate your own way forward because no one else is taking responsibility for where you go.* Corporations and systems used to bear responsibility for certain burdens and risks. Now individuals shoulder the burdens and risks that institutions used to.

4. *You may need to reroute or reconstruct the very river you travel down.* Certain ideological systems and work environments are broken. In this age, it's up to change makers, risk-takers, and the faithful to repair or start fresh when our contexts aren't bearing fruit for the common good.

As you read through this section, try to name how these Big Unspokens impact you. Say out loud how they've shaped what you think is possible and what makes you afraid. Write down the ways you carry the pressure of them in your body and in your heart. Ask God to hold each revelation as you discover it. Add any to the list that are pressing in your own work!

### *Big Unspoken #1: Grab a Paddle Because We've Traded Static Career Paths for Dynamic Ones*

For the cohorts of workers who came of age in mid- to late-twentieth-century America, the road to success might have looked like this: pick an industry, go to school if that industry required it, and more or less count on steady work in your chosen field until you retired. In his book *The Start-Up of You*, Reid Hoffman, the founder of LinkedIn, describes this era of American work like an escalator. People stepped onto the proverbial escalator when they got their first job. Then they presumably took a steady and slow ride up. When they were ready to retire—or hop off the escalator—they did so with a pension and maybe even a gold watch. Importantly, different paths had certain rules about who could get on the escalator and enjoy a ride to the top: some escalators were just for men; some were just for white folks. The paths to success were clear, but they didn't work for everyone.

Today, the escalators aren't really working at all. Hoffman says that they're "jammed at every level." He continues, "Today, it's hard for the young to get on the escalator, it's hard for the middle-aged to ascend, and it's hard for anyone over sixty to get off."[1] People, even the highly educated, are stuck at the bottom without enough work or without work at all. Simultaneously, people in their sixties and seventies without enough money for retirement are staying in or rejoining the workforce.

If Reid Hoffman gives us a picture of how things were in the past, Thomas Friedman gives us an image that captures how things are now. Friedman writes for the *New York Times*, commenting on everything from foreign affairs to the environment to globalization. In his book *Thank You for Being Late*, Friedman helps readers imagine that today's workers are likely to relate to a kayaker moving down a rapids-filled river. Gone are the days of smoothly riding up an escalator; now we're in the midst of raging water!

There are two elements to this kayaker that I want to run with: what's happening in the water and what's happening in the kayak. First, let's unpack the water. Have you ever been white water rafting? I have a couple of times. By far, my most memorable time was on the Ocoee River, a spot just north of Cleveland, Tennessee, that was used for Olympic runs at the 1996 games. The Ocoee was close to my college town, so every summer a handful of friends had summer jobs taking people down the rapids, including my best friend, Jess, who was, in my novice (and wrongheaded) opinion, too petite to be a river guide.

One summer, Jess begged me to go down the river with her. Even beyond my doubt in her physical capacity, I had zero interest in doing so. One word: recirculating. What's this, you ask? Well, there are a couple of rapids on the Ocoee that if a person falls out can trap them in a recirculating pattern. If trapped, you're unable to swim free. No thank you!

Despite my fear, Jess eventually talked me into a ride. I kid you not, I have never in my life listened to any "in case of an emergency" speech with such focus. Alongside fifteen other groups, we were told how to use our bodies to lean with the boat, how to paddle effectively during the rapids, and how to convert our paddle into a rescue line should one of our raft mates fall in. When we were ready to set out, I asked Jess to put me in the safest possible spot, the one least likely to tip out. She obliged.

As our group carried our raft into the still water at the top of the Ocoee, I looked ahead a couple of hundred feet. We had learned in the safety speech that the largest rapid on our trip was the first one we'd make our way through. It was a Class IV rapid with a reputation for recirculating people. We settled in, and I took a deep breath as our boat predictably drifted toward the rapid. But just seconds before the tip of our raft went over the edge of it, the grey-haired man next to me tipped over the side of our raft and into the raging waters. He was about to be swept into the recirculating rapid! Eyes wide with panic, he looked up at me, the only person he could likely see. Fueled by a rush of adrenaline, I spun my paddle around and lunged it toward him. As he grabbed on, I heaved with all my might to pull him into our boat. But my heave had only pulled him near to our boat. He was still destined to ride the rapid in the water attached to our boat only by my oar! Just then, from over my shoulder, I felt Jess's arm reach past mine as she lifted him into the boat with one hand. Yes, one hand! That was the last time I ever doubted the strength of a woman.

Today, people experience the world of work more like navigating down the rushing Ocoee River than riding up an escalator. Changes come often and come fast. Take, for example, the fact that I'm writing this book amid a pandemic. When the stay-at-home orders came, Dan and I, like so many others, started working exclusively from home. Our preschooler started virtual learning via Zoom and Marco

Polo. We took our son to the doctor via a telehealth service. We started to have our groceries delivered thanks to a booming delivery economy. My travel and live-event schedule ground to a halt, while my virtual events picked up speed. Within days, I was on new learning curves for how to lead a team remotely, support my kid in virtual learning, and parent and work simultaneously. The changes felt abrupt, much like going over a Class IV rapid splayed out on the raft, no paddle in hand.

The second part of Friedman's image that I want to unpack is the kayaker. Not unlike the raft I was in, the goal as a kayaker moves over white water rapids is what's called *dynamic stability*. Dynamic stability is the ability to remain in stable motion while on moving (raging!) water. The key to achieving dynamic stability for a kayaker rests in their ability to paddle as fast as or faster than the rapids. If their paddle moves too slowly, it acts like a rudder instead of a paddle, which means that the kayak could turn in an unintended direction and cause destabilization and thus danger. But when the kayaker adjusts their paddling pace to match the pace of the rapids, they are able to move fluidly and with stability in even the strongest of waters.[2]

If our career paths are more dynamic than static, then, like the kayaker, our goal is dynamic stability. We've got to paddle as fast or faster than the rapids. A natural reaction to our sensing this unspoken rule to paddle faster is to do more—to hustle more. And again, hustle can be a valuable approach for certain tasks or seasons. But as a lifestyle, hustle inevitably yields diminishing returns of productivity and well-being. So if not hustle, how do we proverbially paddle *faster*?

We paddle faster by doing two things: (1) embracing quicker cycles of action and reflection (more on this in chapter 11); and (2) prioritizing the skills that enable us to deal with a dynamic and changing world: resilience, creativity, empathy, risk-taking, and reflection (each of these gets its own chapter).

For me, the sobering part of the kayaker analogy is that most kayaks hold only one person. Sometimes they hold two. Kayakers obviously adventure out together, but what happens in one's boat is largely up to that individual. Thank God I had five others in my raft on the Ocoee that day. Thank God I had a competent guide. For as much as I look back on that ride with fondness, the thought of going down that river solo is absolutely terrifying.

When I imagine a seventy-year-old woman, without enough money to retire, strapped into a solo kayak, I honestly want to weep. When I imagine a young man holding a degree in one hand and a paddle in another but without a clue of what's awaiting him around the next bend, I worry. When I picture a parent trying to be present at home while also climbing the professional ladder, I feel overwhelmed at the thought of her going over a Class IV rapid alone. We haven't taught these people all there is to know about navigating the river; we haven't given them the safety speech! The irony? The only safety speech that will truly help is the one that prepares us to be unprepared.

### Big Unspoken #2: Prepare to Be Unprepared Because Change Is Our New Constant Companion

My friend Nathan is a doctor. On his first day of medical school, the dean came in to the lecture hall and welcomed them with these words, "Welcome to your first day of medical school. We're glad you're here. I have some news: 75 percent of what we teach you during these four years will be irrelevant by the time you're out on your own as a doctor. The problem is, we don't know which 75 percent it is. So you're going to need to learn it all and then relearn most of it along the way."

Nathan's story made me think about my own education. I've already said that after grad school, I felt educated but unprepared. But would I say that 75 percent of what I learned feels irrelevant to me today? I honestly don't know. What I can say is that my education probably prepared me for only 25 percent of the things I actually do. That doesn't mean that, like Nathan, 75 percent of the methods I had been trained to use changed by the time I started performing them. But rather that 75 percent of what I do now wasn't covered in the curriculum. I was trained in the Bible, church history, and practical theology and more broadly on how to hold ideas in tension and how to write and communicate. I studied under some phenomenal teachers and thinkers.

But what my degree wasn't designed to help me navigate was change. It wasn't designed to teach me how to articulate fear in the face of the unknown, listen to the deeper layers of conflict, evaluate risk, trust my God-given creativity, accept and adapt to new technology, or collaborate with people who think very differently from me. Those are the lifesaving skills I've had to learn along the way. Partly, people have been learning things "along the way" forever. It's called on-the-job training. But today it seems that some of the skills we find ourselves needing to acquire on the job are less reflective of simply needing practical experience and more so of how different the world is. The differences we feel deep in our bones are the reasons why it's no longer enough to have a good education, technical skills, and a good network. In addition to these, we also need the ability to thrive in the midst of constant change.

Change comes in all shapes and sizes. There's the change that's mostly grief and loss. And there's the change that's mostly hope and opportunity. But in my experience, so much of change is part loss and part opportunity, part grief and part hope. And because of how life works, we often have to wade through loss and opportunity simultaneously. There isn't always time to grieve our expectations or reality as we knew it before we must turn our eyes toward what is next.

Our capacity to grieve loss and seize opportunity simultaneously is as complicated as it sounds. Further complicating all this is that we rarely do all of this work alone. But it's also a wonderfully honest and generative dance. Undergirding this movement is the promise that in God's kingdom, death is not wasted, grief is welcome, and hope and new life have the final word. Because of this, we can trust that God has equipped us to do hard things.

Sifting through what to grieve and developing the instincts to seize opportunity feel a bit like an "eyes to see and ears to hear" situation, which of course makes me think of the parable of the sower. A farmer sowed seeds that fell on different types of land. Some fell on a path and were quickly eaten up by birds. Others fell on rocky soil and had roots too shallow to endure the elements. But the last batch of seed fell on good soil and therefore produced viable crops.

After hearing the story, the disciples come to Jesus and ask, "Why do you speak to the people in parables?" (Matt.

13:10). Jesus explains that when God's message falls on ears that can't hear it, it gets snatched away. When God's message falls on ears that have shallow roots, it won't endure when trouble comes. But when God's Word falls on people who are able to perceive and understand, it yields a fruitful harvest in them.

In a changing world of work, what does it mean to have eyes to see and ears to hear? Preparing to be unprepared—expecting that change will come—can cultivate in us "soil" that's nutrient rich enough to withstand unpredictable weather patterns, pests, and other elements that crops have to endure in order to produce good fruit worth partaking of. Plus, as we allow God to cultivate this type of soil in us, we become hospitable breeding ground for fruit like imagination and risk-taking, empathy and creativity to take root. Each of these fruits are the very skills that will help us make our way to meaningful work in a changing world.

### *Big Unspoken #3: Navigate Your Own Way Forward Because No One Else Is Taking Responsibility for Where You Go*

Abraham is in marketing. He works for a company that promotes events at movie theaters and has been in his position for seven years. Before that he had a similar position at another company for fifteen years. He told me that as he's been shopping his résumé around, the number one piece of feedback he gets is that he hasn't worked in enough places and hasn't had enough diverse experiences. He's been told that today's employers are looking for candidates who have a diversity of skills that they have accumulated across a variety of workplaces, positions, and scenarios. Abraham lamented to me that the advice he'd been given early on was to get in with a good company and climb the ranks. Somewhere along the way that strategy stopped working. He felt as though he'd missed the memo and couldn't go back now and change his earlier approach.

In chapter 1, I likened a person's progress through school to an assembly line. The old way was that kids in school were prepared step-by-step for an escalator workforce. In that age of assembly lines and escalators, decisions about what people worked on and where people worked were made primarily by institutions. Not only this, but systems and institutions shouldered the burden of responsibility for making sure the economy worked, market demands were met, and people were educated and employed. And even more, institutions absorbed certain responsibilities and took on financial risks on behalf of their employees. This applied to benefits such as health care, retirement plans, and life insurance as well as ongoing training and advancement up the escalator.

One clear manifestation of this shift is the rise of the independent economy. An independent worker is any person who gets paid to do something but who is not an official employee of a company. This could include everyone from a rideshare driver to a small-business owner.

We live in an era when it is common for people to have a side hustle or to cobble together a portfolio of work to make a living. Even those of us who are full-time employees move more regularly in and out of gigs and independent work than was true a decade ago.

One chief feature of the independent economy is that individuals shoulder burdens for realities that larger corporations used to. I'm thinking of Donna, who is a voice-over artist for film and television. She got her start on commercials in Los Angeles. She had several successful commercials and was even in a couple of feature films. Then when her kids were young she decided to take five years off. She told me that she recently got in touch with her agent, excited to go on some auditions. Her agent's first direction was, "We need to work on your Instagram following. A lot has changed in five years. Today, it's all about having your own built-in audience."

Though Donna had always worked as a gig worker, she told me that returning to the business after a five-year break made her feel as if she'd been gone for twenty! Now she had to be good not only at her craft but also at marketing herself on social media. And because she was hiring a social media consultant to help her grow her audience, it was costing her money to relearn how to do the thing she had previously done successfully for years. The pressure Donna felt to bear the burden of responsibility for a fan base eventually felt like too much and that it was unfair. She decided it wasn't worth it and gave up voice acting. Maybe you too have felt the pressure to take on new and challenging work just to stay current. Maybe you too have felt new burdens for realities that used to be someone else's responsibilities.

Increasingly, individuals are responsible for navigating their own way forward, whether that includes learning new skills or cultivating a diverse work portfolio or even more practical considerations such as health insurance and retirement. Individuals are doing the work that systems used to do. We need to name this as the mentally demanding reality that it is. And we need to explore how a strong undercurrent of change has fueled all the shifts we're facing.

### *Big Unspoken #4: You May Need to Reroute or Reconstruct the Very River You Travel Down*

We walk through the world with the weight of broken systems on our shoulders. Sometimes it's the invisible glass ceiling that we can't seem to crack through. Other times it's a work-around-the-clock environment that costs us our sleep and our sanity. Or it's the way people talk to one another or what we deem as funny. On any given day, broken systems impact our daily work. Bearing the pressure for how to navigate them is an unspoken weight many of us carry.

Take Luna, for example. When Luna and I met for lunch, she told me she had been working at her nonprofit for five years. In that time period, two of her white male colleagues had been promoted into leadership positions. When I asked Luna if she had ever talked to her boss (also a white man) about a promotion, she said that my strategy might work for me as a white lady, but it wouldn't be as effective for her as a woman of color. She helped me to understand the culture of her office, one that is reflective of so many work environments. From the systemic bias of what good leadership is (and therefore who is fit for it) to the informal dynamics and expectations between her and her boss, I learned why it wasn't so easy as simply asking for a raise.

Luna was faced with a tough decision. Should she seek to reform the organization? That task would surely come with intense mental and emotional load and may or may not be effective. Should she look for a new job? Potentially that would mean making a lateral move in title and pay even though she really did deserve to be at the next level in the organization.

If we breathe the air of broken systems too long, they indeed become toxic. This is how my friend James described his work environment. James worked for a global company that hosts large-scale live events. In the weeks leading up to the events, he said it's normal for people to pull sixteen-hour days. And if someone went to dinner with a friend or to their kid's T-ball game, it was normal for the boss to broadcast that the person taking a break was causing more work for everyone else. In this way, people were discouraged from having any kind of boundaries with work.

Now, live events is an industry in which there are unique, last-minute demands. But having witnessed the cycle many times, James reported that many of the issues came down to lack of foresight, poor project management, and a cultural value for profit over people.

Like Luna, James was faced with a series of choices. Did he speak up? If so, what should he say? Should he look for a new job? If so, would he have to start over in terms of relationships and work experience?

And what about all the people who worked alongside Luna and James? What should they do? What was their role in calling out, changing, and potentially redeeming broken systems? Figuring out what work is ours to do is risky and intimidating and often unspoken. And, much of the time, the choice about how to engage isn't always clear.

Sometimes it's the case that we need to stay and help to redeem broken systems. Other times that's absolutely not our work to do. Regularly living in these tensions constantly demands that we use our energy to decide what to do and how to do it, and to hope that we've made the right decisions.

## Making Sense of Change

Given these Big Unspokens (and the inevitable others that aren't covered here), there is a sense of urgency around our developing the skills to make it down the river in one piece and, whenever possible, to move from surviving to thriving. Both for the sake of ourselves and others. Let me suggest that in order to survive and thrive, we can do three things: (1) get "good enough" at reading the rapids, (2) lean in and let go in the face of change, and (3) let water off your boat.

### Get "Good Enough" at Reading the Rapids

As we stare down the rapids that await us, our livelihoods depend on our capacity to get good enough at reading the river. Put another way: we've got to get good enough at making sense of the currents of change that impact our life and work. How do we get "good enough"?

Getting good enough at reading change means that we learn both what to pay attention to and how to pay attention. We learn to make a connection between what we're experiencing and the fact that the world is moving both closer together and further apart at the same time.

It means that we grow in our capacity to describe how our awesome but also overwhelming access to everything from politics to finances feels. On the one hand, it's truly amazing that we can talk to one another, trade with one another, and travel to one another in ways unlike previous generations. On the other hand, increased access in the midst of accelerated technology can have a fracturing effect. It enables a kind of hunkering down into our own way of seeing the world as our opinions and viewpoints are reinforced by news and information tailored to us.

Getting good enough at reading change means that we're able to step back and name how the giant factors such as globalization, climate change, accelerated technology, and crumbling ideologies impact our everyday lives and work. Important in all this is that we're able to identify the difference between changes that are happening to us and changes that we need to make. We must also be able to identify those changes we can make fairly easily and those that will require us to see and embrace the world in new ways. The changes that require us to see the world in new ways often take quite a bit of listening to others, attunement to God, and resilience as we navigate the way forward alongside others.

In a seminal book on change, Harvard professors Ronald Heifetz and Marty Linksy distinguish between two types of challenges: technical and adaptive. Technical challenges are problems that have clear (even if complex) solutions or that can be solved by experts or through established patterns.[3] Adaptive challenges, on the other hand, are ones that have unclear solutions and often require a value shift in order to make change happen. They're fuzzier, more painful, and slow going because they require people to wrestle with deeply held assumptions and to experiment with new ways of being.[4]

The ability to read the rapids and to perceive opportunity in the midst of change are almost always adaptive challenges that require adaptive skills, such as creativity and resilience, empathy and imagination. The good news is that we can indeed cultivate the skills to get good enough at reading the rapids before us.

At the heart of cultivating adaptive skills and getting good enough at reading the rapids is the capacity to lean in and let go while also somehow being tethered so that we're not swept away.

### Lean In and Let Go

We're riding down white water rapids in a kayak by ourselves. Giant forces far beyond our control fuel those rapids. Change—and accelerated change at that—is the only predictable future. What do we do? I want to suggest that we develop the capacity to lean in and let go so that we may harness the momentum of change. Let me illustrate this with two stories.

Several years ago, Dan and I were driving in our trusty SUV to a friend's house to watch March Madness. We were only a half mile from our house when a large truck turned left and into the side of our car. The impact was so intense that our car flipped on its head. All our windows were shattered, the roof was smashed in, and we were hanging upside down, strapped in by our seat belts. My window was too compressed to escape from. A man whose name I'll never know pulled us out of the driver's side window, and we were rushed to the trauma center of our local hospital.

Right before we were hit, time seemed to stand still. I can still remember feeling like I was waiting to get hit. I can still remember bracing myself for the crash. I don't understand how so much happened in that millisecond. But as I've talked with other crash victims since, I've learned that it's a common experience. Time does, for whatever reason, seem to stand still.

In that millisecond before the impact, Dan turned to me and said, "We're about to get hit. Lean in and let go!"

His advice was that of a skier who had been trained to fall. Dan grew up skiing in the Salt Lake area and has explained to me that one of the chief goals when learning to ski is to learn how to fall and to excel at the same time—kind of like learning to grieve and seize opportunity at the same time. He says it's as if he learned to fall on the mountain before he learned to ski it. Falling requires letting go and relaxing your body. If you tense up or try to catch yourself along the way, your tighter muscles lead to more pain. But if you lean in and let go, you can endure most of what can happen when you fall.

Ironically, as skiers learn to let go in a fall, they develop the capacity to become more attuned to the momentum of their bodies and thus can potentially position themselves both physically and mentally. By letting go and tuning in to their bodies, they have a better chance of pulling their skis underneath them or recovering. Resisting the fall shortcuts the attunement necessary to bounce back.

Another way to think about this is that learning to fall helps us cultivate an instinct found in squirrels and cats. Have you ever noticed that these animals always land on their feet? That's because the second they fall, their brains feel the momentum and they instantly calculate exactly where they are going to land. They actually turn their heads to look right at the landing spot and start positioning their bodies, *using* the momentum to land.

By becoming less afraid to fall (or to hit rapids head-on), we can develop the instinct to "land on our feet." In this way, we move beyond just enduring change or bracing for impact. We move to leverage the moments of impact for our way forward.

When Dan skis down a mountain, he does so at blazing speed. (By the way, yes, I am looking for a partner who wants to join me on the bunny slopes and drink copious amounts of hot chocolate on long breaks in the lodge.) When Dan is going that fast, he describes having to quickly calculate what to do with many changes or setbacks. A ski suddenly slips out or, even worse, gets caught up on something, and suddenly he's got one ski facing the entirely wrong direction. To mix metaphors, he encounters a lot of rapids going down the mountain. But he's hit those unpredictable moments enough times that he is now prepared to be unprepared. He's able to use his momentum, adapt, or fall and recover.

In the millisecond before our SUV got hit, I did not let go. I did not sense the momentum of my body like an expert skier or a mad-eyed squirrel. No, I tensed up and braced myself. Dan's learned skills enabled him to not only endure the impact but also perform well under pressure by looking out for me. Many years later, I have ongoing pain from that crash; Dan has none. I'm convinced it's because in the face of impact, I tensed up while he leaned in and let go.

What does it look like to lean in, let go, and harness the momentum of change in our work?

After graduation, Dan and I pieced together odd jobs. I worked a bit for my aunt and took on some copywriting gigs. Dan edited videos for a small production company. We were underemployed, almost broke, and stressed. We quickly found ourselves with more bills than we could pay.

Six months into our underemployment and mounting debt, we got two calls that would impact how we approached the next season of our careers. The first was from one of my seminary professors. He knew I was jobless and wondered if I would help an organization he worked with to develop a simple keynote presentation. The other call was from an interior designer friend of my father's. She wanted to know if Dan would help her make a video. Driven by financial necessity, we immediately said yes to both opportunities. As we were doing the projects, we heard from both of our "clients" about how relieved they were to find someone who could do these creative jobs.

Hearing their sense of relief made me wonder if there was a business opportunity there. So after the projects were finished, we decided we should experiment with doing "creative work" as a way to make some money. We quickly put together a website and sent a note to family and friends, asking them to file us in their mental file folders under graphic design, videos, and websites. Our small experiment landed us a few more projects, which in time snowballed into a few bigger projects. Before we knew it, our little side hustle was an actual business.

I never imagined myself running a creative agency. I've already mentioned that I thought I'd find work with a world-changing nonprofit. When we started our business, I had zero skills in branding, film, or even the operational parts of running a business. As I had zero skills, you can imagine how many times I fell on the mountain while learning the basics. Not having technical skills also meant that neither passion nor competency were key motivators for me. Instead, my motivations were basic financial need and the desire to harness what felt like natural momentum from those first two clients. I suppose in this way, I am a bit like the mad-eyed squirrel in that I learned to harness the momentum of change and land on my feet.

As my work evolved into helping people wrestle honestly with their biggest questions of career and calling, I've witnessed much variation in our collective capacity to lean in and let go—to harness the momentum of change. Sometimes we tense up and brace ourselves. Sometimes we land on our feet. Cultivating the instinct[5] to harness the momentum of change is not a skill we learn once. Like kayaking or skiing, it's a skill we must regularly practice to stay sharp.

### Let Water off Your Boat

Sometimes, even though we're doing all we can to read the rapids and to lean in and let go, we still take on water. It just happens.

When my son was two months old, we had a friend temporarily move in with us. She was separating from her wife and needed somewhere to land. Nearly every day, I'd sit holding and feeding my baby while listening to my friend talk about overwhelmingly hard things. After many days of this rhythm, I sort of broke down. I was already tired from mothering my children, and as badly as I wanted to be the best friend my friend needed, I was running out of capacity to do much of anything.

I called my mom, who always listens to me for as long as I need to be heard. I asked her how I could be both a good mother and a good friend but also good to myself in this stretch. She spoke over me a truth I have echoed to countless people since: "You're taking on a lot of water. In order not to drown, you've got to intentionally let water off your boat." If you've ever been in a boat, a raft, or a kayak, you know that taking on water is less than ideal. Having clear strategies for getting the water off are critical to survival.

Despite learning how to read the rapids and how to lean in and let go, we're still sometimes going to take on water. It's just part of what it means to be a people living in the Age of Overwhelm. It's also true that each of us has our own triggers. It's important to identify when we take on water and how we let it off.

## EXERCISE: Let Water off Your Boat

You're going to make two lists: one to identify when you take on water and one to identify how you let water off your boat. Note that in this exercise, we're not yet trying to avoid taking on water but instead starting with the premise that we inevitably take some on. Certain kinds of water might be better to avoid taking on (e.g., a toxic relationship at work), but others are necessary for growth and change (e.g., increased exposure to the realities of racism for people in particular sociocultural locations).

To identify when you take on water and how you let it off your boat, take the following steps:

1. Reflect on your work over the past month or so. It might help you to look back over your calendar or your to-do list to get a sense of the people you engaged with and the projects you worked on. If your work has regular rhythms to it, think about the tasks you do and the people you engage with regularly.

2. Make a list of when you felt like you were taking on water—when you felt overwhelmed or stressed or just

too full. Those feelings of taking on water can come from external forces or from within. Try to be specific. For example, every time I talk to Jim at work, all he does is complain; I leave feeling overwhelmed. Or, I took on water when I had to do the financial reports in a new way—that just doesn't feel like my sweet spot. Or, we've got so many changing protocols at work, and I'm expected to lead people through them when I don't even understand them myself.

3. Now reflect on your life beyond your work over the past month or so. Again, it might help to look back over your calendar to be reminded of the things you spent time doing, places you went, or people you saw.

4. Again, make a list of when you felt like you were taking on water—when you felt overwhelmed or stressed or just too full. Try to be specific. For example, I feel like I'm taking on water when I read the news or when I have a difficult conversation with a friend.

5. Now make a list of the things you do that help you feel like you're letting water off the boat. These can be habitual practices or things you do more randomly. For example, I go for a jog, I cook a meal, I call a friend, or I meditate for fifteen minutes.

6. Compare your lists. Are there themes in regard to what causes you to feel like you're taking on water? Are there themes that emerge in regard to what helps you feel like you're letting water off the boat?

7. Highlight or circle what feel like the three most pressing times you're taking on water, whether in your work or personal life. Highlight or circle what feel

like the three most effective ways to let water off your boat.

8. Finally, commit to pair up when you're taking on water with how you might let water off the boat. For example, when I have a difficult conversation with a coworker, I'll go on a fifteen-minute walk with my headphones in. Or, when I spend a frustrating day learning a new skill, I'll have a mini dance party. Record these commitments somehow and experiment with putting them into practice this week.

# 3

# Believe That You
# Are Called

Recently, I had separate conversations with two friends who were in career crises. Each crisis was catalyzed by a sense of disillusionment with their work—the feeling that the world had promised them something and was failing to make good on that promise.

One friend, in her midthirties, is in the midst of a corporate career climb. She's smart, kind, and works hard to jump through the hoops of her work's corporate culture. She's been promoted twice in the last year, each promotion coming with a larger portfolio of work, more autonomy, and more money.

One day, she texted me on the verge of another promotion. She gave me the details and I sent back the most celebratory

GIFs I could find. But then she abruptly pivoted from excitement to what seemed like intense anxiety and unhappiness. I was taken aback. She helped me to see that just as she was rearing back to jump through yet another hoop, she had a sinking feeling that she didn't actually care about her work—at all. She enjoyed receiving the promotions and had friendships among her colleagues, but she didn't like the work. She described it as "soul sucking." She was anxious because she was used to making good money and had bought a house with her husband, so she didn't feel it was possible to start over. She'd be a decade behind in any new industry. Exasperated, she wrote, "It's hard, because I'm doing all the things I was supposed to, but I'm just not happy."

My other friend is earlier in his career. He graduated college two years ago. In the short time since, he has come face-to-face with the reality that a degree from a good school does not equal a job where the people are nice and the work is meaningful. When we met for coffee, he told me how horrible his boss was and how that was apparently just part of the industry. I asked him if there was anything about his work that was satisfying or enjoyable. He leaned in and almost whispered across the table, "I feel like the degree I got was pointless. And I feel like a failure because I have a crappy job. And I don't even want to tell my mom because she's so proud of me."

Let me get one thing out of the way: sometimes work just sucks. It can be demanding and exhausting and about as far from fun as you might imagine.

Now that that's out of the way, let's talk about how pervasive disillusionment about work is. And how that disillusionment sets us up for unhappiness. We've been indoctrinated to have particular types of hopes and expectations about our work. So when work doesn't play out as expected, it's no wonder we're unhappy.

One example of this kind of indoctrination can be found in Christian circles. There is a Bible verse that is used, abused, and plastered on graduation cards for high school and college across the United States. It reads, "For surely I know the plans I have for you, says the LORD, plans for your welfare and not for harm, to give you a future with hope" (Jer. 29:11). I remember seeing it on my own college graduation gifts and how it inspired me and made me feel as though God had a unique path just for me. At the time, I never bothered to read the verse in context. If I had, I would have known that the writer likely never intended it for graduation gifts!

More accurately, the verse is part of a larger text meant to sustain an entire community in exile—to assure them that God has not forgotten them. Jeremiah 29 was written for people who had to flee their homes in fear and then make their way through a scary and unknown land. It wasn't for individual people picking a career path. It didn't have anything to do with personal passion. Our appropriation of this text for career sentiments is a symptom of an overly individualistic expression of Christianity. It's a painful example of how the Christian faith has been relegated to individual aspects of people's lives amid a changing world.[1] Plus, it signals that we have much unlearning to do when it comes to calibrating our imaginations for the way forward. Central to unlearning is dealing with the dysfunctional beliefs that govern our current hopes and expectations.

## Dealing with Dysfunction[2]

As I've talked with hundreds of people trying to make their way in a new world of work, I've learned that misuse of Jeremiah 29:11 is not the only underlying narrative causing disillusionment and thus dissatisfaction. Whenever I teach a class, I have students work to identify the dysfunctional beliefs they might be trapped within. I've heard at least fifty different dysfunctional beliefs. I'm sure you have your own list. Following are three common ones. See if you can identify yourself as you read through them.

### Dysfunctional Belief #1: Passion Is the Holy Grail of Work

We are inundated with messages about finding work we are passionate about. From college commencement speeches to career counseling to casual conversations with friends, the advice we too often give one another is about finding our passions and then deciding on work that lets us fulfill those passions.

In a recent Pew report, 95 percent of teenagers say that having a job or career they enjoy is the top priority for their future. This priority comes over helping others, having a lot of money, getting married, having children, or becoming famous.[3] From an early age, individuals are developing a vision for their work that hinges completely on their personal passions and loves.

This is problematic. First, it reflects a very privileged approach to work accessible only to those for whom the rules of society most favor. It's just not the case that most of us get to decide what we do for work based on a rubric of passion and love. Plus, thinking about calling as a job we're passionate about negates the role of work in much of the world and throughout most of human history. I think about people in farming societies whose work is defined by the land and by community. Or parents whose work is to care for small children. Maybe these farmers or parents in fact love their work, but personal passion is likely not the prerequisite for what they do.

Even for those of us who have more space to consider what we love as we work, trying to pin down what we're passionate about is often much harder than it sounds. In fact, trying to first find what we love to do and then find work that matches it threatens to thwart professional development, discovery, and discernment.

Several years ago, I was in Florida teaching a class about vocation to a group of graduate students. I had given birth to my first child just ten weeks earlier, so I was a sleepless, foggy-brained mess. In one class session, I remember running my hands through my greasy hair, rubbing my eyes, and fumbling over my words. I was trying to find language to explain what a sacred experience leaping before we looked had been when we first started Long Winter Media.

And then I saw him. Set against a backdrop of white sand and bright blue sky was a man wearing oversized headphones and clutching a metal detector with both hands. Head lowered, he made his way down the beach, waving the machine methodically back and forth in search of valuables. I motioned to my class to take a look, and as we did, we talked together about how easy it is for us to treat God's callings like special treasures waiting to be uncovered in the sand.

Callings from God are less like treasures waiting to be uncovered in the sand and more like slabs of marble waiting to be chiseled away over time.[4] What this means is that instead of thinking we've got to know our passions and do work that matches them, we can instead lean into a God who is lovingly shaping and forming us along the way for all that we might be called to do and become.

### Dysfunctional Belief #2: We Are What We Do

I am in the stage of life when I go to a lot of kids' birthday parties. Whenever I'm at a party where I don't know many people, I revert back to my awkward middle school self. Not wanting to hover near my kid and not quite able to jump into adult conversations, I linger by the drink table. I was in the midst of pouring a cup of coffee and giving my inner middle schooler a pep talk about being brave when another mom bounded over to me in the way only an extreme extrovert is comfortable enough to do. She introduced herself as Jen. We talked for a while about our kids and the impressive mermaid-themed birthday party. And then, when there was a lull in the conversation, I asked her the first question that came to my mind: "So what do you do?"

Jen responded, "I took some time off with the kids and now I'm in between things and it's time to do something but I'm just not quite sure what and ugh! It's actually kind of embarrassing—I'm a forty-year-old woman and I don't know what I want to be when I grow up. I'm not totally sure what my calling is." In three sentences, her tone had moved from bubbly conversationalist to uncertainty with a hint of shame.

I knew better. I shouldn't have asked her that question, at least not like that. Over time, I've had enough turbulent conversations with people in transitions, people who don't like their jobs, or people who aren't making money by doing things they like that I should've known better. I should've known asking, What do you do? can feel more like shame bait than an invitation for friendship.

I've thought a lot about why the question feels like such a trap. Why might what we do—or don't do—prompt shame? In trying to untangle it all, an image from my childhood comes to mind: the tabernacle that sat on the altar of the Catholic church I grew up in. Not that the altar is a place of shame. Hear me out. If you have ever been inside a Catholic church, you know that there is always an altar at the front—a physical place where the most sacred elements of the worshiping body are located. It's also where the celebration of Mass takes place. On the altar of my home church, there was an ornate tabernacle. It's beauty was for me a visual cue that the Eucharist we kept inside of it was of great value to our community.

We are a species built for worship. And whether we can see it or not, we worship more than just God. Our sometimes shame (or on the flip side, pride) at answering the question, What do you do? makes me wonder, *Do we worship work? Do we collectively idolize work as a pathway to personal significance and as a way to define ourselves? Is it a means through which we as individuals feel glorified?* On this, Derek Thompson, a writer for the *Atlantic*, writes about what might be called the religion of workism: "What is workism? It is the belief that work is not only necessary to economic production but also the centerpiece of one's identity and life's purpose."[5]

Just like any religion, we make altars to what we love. On our collective altar of work, we find things such as production and wealth, white collars, and long hours. We find systems such as white supremacy and patriarchy—realities that work for some and alienate others. And inside the tabernacle?

Inside we find calling conflated with capitalism. Inside we find a mantra that tells us we are special and valuable because of what we get paid to do. And then I wonder, *Do we worship work, or do we worship ourselves?* We feel the pressure for our work to not only be significant but also help us feel significant. It makes sense, then, that if we in any way feel distant from the altar that society worships, we feel shame. It makes sense that Jen fumbled over her words and didn't quite know what to do with the "What do you do?" question. Capitalism was never meant to be our vehicle for calling. Work was never meant to save us. Though our work has deep and meaningful implications in the kingdom of God, our sense of significance can't be reduced to what we do for work.

### Dysfunctional Belief #3: It All Happens Right Away

My husband is a filmmaker. When he was first getting into the film industry, a mentor gave him the following advice: "It'll take ten years before you're actually doing what you think you're going to be doing tomorrow." Not a decade to become famous or rich or accomplish one's career dreams. No, a decade just to have steady work doing what he could already imagine doing.

At first, this advice felt like a punch in the gut. That's because it felt so contrary to what we both imagined to be true about calling. Namely, we thought that because we sensed God calling us to particular kinds of work, our careers would unfold smoothly and without major obstacles. Now almost a decade later, I realize just how wrong we were. Of course things don't happen right away. Of course there are obstacles and surprises along the way.

For some of us, obstacles take the shape of the hardships that come with missed opportunities or lack of direction. For others, systemic realities of inequity or marginalization seem to rear their head around every corner.

Part of accepting that it doesn't all happen right away comes when we make peace with the fact that God doesn't promise smooth vocational journeys. If anything, Scripture teaches us to expect the unexpected and to ready ourselves for difficulty, reminding us that God's timing is such a critical component of calling. Biblical figures such as Moses and Joseph sensed God's calling and then had to journey for quite some time before seeing it realized. When we miss the reality that God guides us on vocational journeys, we miss all the formation God does as our sense of calling takes shape.

Nearly a decade later, it's shocking to me how true those words were from my husband's mentor—for both my husband's career and my own. I am finally doing some of what I imagined myself doing back then. I'm also doing a lot of things I never imagined myself doing. Ironically, just as I'm stepping into new opportunities, God is forming my imagination for what might unfold over the next decade. In this, I am learning to play the long game of vocation.

So how did we get here? How did we arrive at the place where dysfunction is our guiding light?

## Riding the Fumes of Reformation Theology

I am no stranger to the gas warning light in my car. I tell myself that the little orange icon on the dashboard is an inexcusable sight for a woman in her late thirties—and doubly off-limits for a mother of two.

But the gas light does not listen. It pops up on my dashboard whether I like it or not. After all, it's there to warn me, to protect us. Sometimes when I see it, I head straight to the station, but most of the time it's not convenient to stop. I can't possibly stop with restless kids in the car or when I'm late for an important meeting. So I push it further. Inevitably, I am riding on fumes, praying that I've got just a bit more time before I run out of gas.

Sisters and brothers, when it comes to a theology of calling, the gas light has been on for a while. The last time we really filled up was the Protestant Reformation. Yet here we are five hundred years later, riding on the fumes of old thinking. Let me be clear, old theology does not automatically mean bad theology. It's just that theology is always contextual. In this case, theology that was absolutely liberating in sixteenth-century Europe still holds up in some ways. But in other ways, it is incredibly limiting for twenty-first-century America.

### Before the Protestant Reformation

In order to understand why what was liberating then is limiting now, we've got to know a bit about the historical context of the Reformation. Stay with me here. Theologian William Placher has a wonderful book that traces how the Western Christian theology of vocation (which is just another word for calling) evolved through the ages. Placher starts with the early church, the period of time right after Jesus's death and resurrection when the Roman Empire expected its citizens to pledge allegiance to the imperial cult. To even admit that one was a Christian was a move that came with serious risks of physical harm, arrest, and even death. The theology of calling centered on the sole question, Should I be a Christian? Calling didn't have anything to do with people's paid work but rather their central allegiance to Christ.

Then, as things often do, questions of calling shifted in the fourth century after the Christian conversion of the Roman Emperor Constantine. Now the most powerful person in the land was Christian! This meant that to claim Christ as Messiah was no longer risky. In fact, it was popular. When this happened, some worried that the risk and sacrifice that had been central to Christianity would cease to exist. This fear gave rise to early monasticism, including the fleeing of some from population centers out to the desert to live lives marked by sacrifice and risk in the name of Jesus. So in this era, which Placher broadly categorizes as the Middle Ages, the central question about calling shifted from, Should I be a Christian? to, What kind of a Christian should I be?[6]

In this time period, Christians grabbed hold of the idea that to have a calling from God meant to have a special call to spiritual work. If people were called to be a monk or a priest, they had this spiritually significant calling. Everyone else did not. Sadly, there are pervasive remnants of this age-old hierarchy in certain Christian circles today.

### *How Martin Luther Shaped Today's Conversation on Calling*

The Middle Ages eventually gave way to the Reformation era. Martin Luther is one of the most iconic figures of the Reformation. He challenged the church on so much, including how it thought about calling. Luther observed that people's attempt to reclaim sacrifice as central to calling had produced arrogant priests and monks who thought their work was more spiritually significant than that of everyday people. Luther rejected the idea that only certain roles in society were spiritually significant.

Luther's pushback on the church in the Reformation era sets the foundation for the way much of Western Christianity understands theology today. Let's unpack it a bit more. Luther wrote in reaction to the theology of calling developed in the Middle Ages. Again, there were basically two life paths: stay part of one's family, taking on the work obligations associated with it, and get married and have kids; or have a *vocation*, which meant becoming a priest, monk, or nun.[7] To choose the latter was thought to have an elevated spiritual status with God. Everyone else's work—the parent, the baker, the farmer—was thought to be spiritually insignificant.[8] Luther (and other Reformers) rejected the idea that only certain jobs held spiritual status with God. He argued that every role, which he called a *station*, had the capacity to be meaningful in the kingdom.

Rooted in his readings of Paul, Martin Luther rejected the idea that a person can secure salvation through the efforts of their own hands.[9] For Luther, the mystery and the beauty of God's grace is that it's not earned. God's grace is a gift. As Luther's ideas started to spread, people called into question the previous thinking that the primary purpose of our living and working was to perform good deeds so that we might earn favor with God and make our way to heaven. If daily work was no longer a vehicle to shore up good deeds to go to heaven, then what was it? Luther offered that the purpose of daily work was to be in loving service to our neighbors through one's particular station. The bread the baker baked, the medicine the apothecaries mixed, the sermon the preacher preached—all of it was an opportunity to live in loving service to one's neighbor.

For Luther, all Christians have a *spiritual call* to have faith in and love for God and also an *external call* to love our neighbors through our particular station.[10] In the wake of Luther's reframing theology, the central vocational question for people became, How do I love and serve my neighbor from the station where God has placed me?

Theology is always contextual. In order to appreciate just how liberating Luther's work was, it's important to understand that he was writing to people in an agrarian economy, which simply means that they worked the land and that commerce and life were shaped mostly by agriculture and farming. People were born into family trades and often remained in those stations their entire lives. It was not at all common to change jobs or move to a new place for work. So when Luther basically says, "Hey, you don't have to leave your station to do something that matters to God; in fact, God wants you to remain in your station and love and serve your neighbor right where you are," it liberates people to think in new ways about how their work matters to God.

Then industrialization happened. Machines disrupted nearly every aspect of life and work. The disruption brought certain ways of life to a halt and at the same time opened up new opportunities. One of the results was that people no longer remained in singular stations for the entirety of their working years. It was now possible for people to move from towns to cities and take on jobs outside of the family trade. Yet we held on to a theology that equates one's static economic role with one's sense of calling. As we traded more permanent stations for jobs and eventually careers, the implied equation became *calling = job*.

This theology was in use for a couple hundred years until the dawn of the Information Age. Just as machines disrupted the agrarian lifestyle, so too did the Information Age disrupt the industrial way of being. In the Information Age, with seemingly endless possibilities in front of us, our implied equation for calling has shifted once again. Instead of calling = the invitation to follow Christ (as in the early church), or calling = a professional Christian (as in the Middle Ages), or calling = loving service to my neighbor from within my station (as in the Reformation era), our definitions of calling are more like calling = a job I love, calling = my purpose, or calling = the work I can't not do.

Starting with the early church, much of the human quest around vocation has been to define a theology of calling in a way that sets Christians apart from others spiritually—something that makes us unique. The tricky part was when our work became overly conflated with this theology of calling. The Reformation pushed back on that impulse in a really helpful way but reinforced it in another. Today, when we make our jobs and capitalism the places where our set-apartness ought to be expressed, we're in for disappointment. We end up thinking that callings are jobs that we love or places where we get to live out our passions. Remember, capitalism was never meant to be a vehicle for calling.

Of course, passion isn't bad; in fact, it's beautiful and good. But it's not nearly a wide enough container to hold all that God calls us to. We need to trade any definition of calling that promotes hyperindividualism or is overly enmeshed with capitalism for one that reflects a biblical perspective and considers our context of a changing world of work.

## Nesting Dolls of Calling

Some of the most influential work on calling was done in a time period when commerce was almost exclusively local and people's work was fairly fixed. Today, neither of those things is true. We live in a globalized world where not only do people change jobs often but also the very work we deem as necessary to function as a society is evolving all the time. The fact that our theology in use can be traced to ideas meant for a very different context is part of the reason why dysfunctional beliefs hold us back and short-circuit our opportunities to meaningfully participate with God in the world through our work.

It has been helpful for me to think about calling like a set of nesting dolls. Picture with me a traditional Russian set, hand decorated with a pale-faced, rosy-cheeked woman with perfectly parted black hair. She's wearing a pink and red ornamental dress, which is covered in detailed white flowers. When you open the first doll, you're met with another doll featuring the exact same woman, only smaller. You keep opening them until you hold the smallest, innermost one in the palm of your hand.

I think calling is a lot like a set of nesting dolls. We have an innermost calling from God—the most sacred and core calling to belong to Jesus. From there, more nesting dolls are added, each representing another layer of God's calling to us. I want to suggest four layers of God's calling: the call to belong to Christ, the call to work toward redemption, the call to create, and the call to particulars.

### *The First and Innermost Doll: The Call to Belong to Christ*

God's most central call to us is to belong to Jesus Christ. Full stop. This call from God to us is both an individual and a collective call. Meaning that it's fully ours to own, but not just ours to own, and that the fullness of this call comes to life in the presence of community. When we answer God's innermost call to belong, we are grafted into a family— sisters and brothers who, like us, are called to belong to God. Together, as the church, we are called to be Christ's holy people, called to follow Jesus together.[11]

In the Gospels, we catch a glimpse of this innermost call as Jesus repeatedly beckons his disciples to literally follow him. We see it in Matthew 4 when on the shore of the Sea of Galilee Jesus calls out to the brothers Peter and Andrew to follow him, and they leave their nets and follow. We see it in Luke 5 when Jesus calls Levi the tax collector to follow him, and he gets out of his tax booth and follows.[12]

The call to follow Jesus is not just about physically walking behind Jesus as Peter, Andrew, and Levi did. It's about identifying as a follower of Jesus in all we do. It's about actively belonging to Jesus and letting that belonging shape everything we do.

In Mark 3, Jesus calls his twelve disciples to come and be with him so that he may send them out into the world to do the work of the kingdom. We read, "Jesus went up on a mountainside and called to him those he wanted, and they came to him. He appointed twelve that they might *be with him* and that he might send them out" (vv. 13–14, emphasis added). In the Gospels, following or being with Jesus often meant a new way of living that stood in stark contrast to a person's old life. Jesus commanded people to leave their work, sell their belongings, and reprioritize their relationships. Their lives were to be radically reoriented by the Good News of the kingdom of God in all they did.

Though we cannot literally walk behind the living, breathing Jesus, we too are called to follow him by belonging to him and radically reorienting our lives to kingdom priorities. We are to walk through the world loving God, prioritizing mercy, loving our neighbors, centering marginalized people, practicing forgiveness, extending grace, and living generously with the narrative of Christ as our guiding light.

What does it look like for us to radically realign our lives to follow Jesus? Sometimes it means that we indeed must drastically shift our lifestyles or our priorities when we hear the call of God. But much of the time the radical nature of our reorienting comes in how fervently and regularly we align and realign with the mission of God in all that we do.

*We're called to follow Jesus.*

### The Second Doll: The Call to Work toward Redemption

Not only are we called to belong to Jesus; we are also called to represent Christ in his work of redemption in the world. Though patterns of redemption are found throughout Scripture, the language for my framing of this call comes from 2 Corinthians 5:16–21. This passage tells us that God reconciled the world to himself through Jesus. And that we're to be Christ's ambassadors in God's ongoing ministry of reconciliation in the world—working on behalf of Jesus toward God's priorities of healing, redemption, and shalom. This is mind-blowing to me. It's why I think the call to participate in God's redemption in the world as ambassadors of Christ is the great honor and great challenge of being a Christian. The idea that God is at work converting loss into hope, pain into glory, and betrayal into forgiveness and that we've got a part to play? That's both inspiring and terrifying at the same time.

As with the innermost doll, God's call to participate in redemption is not just for some of us; it's for all of us. It's not just for the individual; it's for the church. It's not a sometimes, some-days, when-we-feel-like-it call. No, it's an all-the-time, all-the-days, no-matter-if-we're-passionate call.

The call to represent Christ and participate in God's mission of redemption is to permeate everything we put our hearts, minds, and hands to. It is to illuminate the way we talk to our coworkers, the way we fight with our spouse, how we manage our time, the projects we commit our energy to, and our visions for the future. In all that we do, we're called to work toward God's mission of redemption in the world.

*We're called to belong to Jesus by joining God's ongoing redemption of the world.*

### The Third Doll: The Call to Create

We're called to create. Our very first story about God is a poem about God's creativity. In Genesis 1, we come to know who God is through a picture of God as maker. God creates the heavens and the earth and separates the night from day. God breathes life into existence by putting birds in the sky and fish in the sea. The cadence of God's creating is broken up only by God's delight in what is unfolding. The poet captures this delight with the phrase, "And God saw that it was good" (v. 10). Creation is good.

After we experience God as creator, God makes humans. The poet writes, "So God created humankind in his own image, in the image of God he created them; male and female he created them" (v. 27). This is honestly kind of unbelievable. We've just learned about God by imagining how God created the whole world in awesome fashion. Then we learn that we are made to reflect the essence of the God who created us. Then God goes on to bless the first people and make what is implicit explicit by commissioning them for their way forward: "Be fruitful and multiply; fill the earth and subdue it" (v. 28). In the most literal sense, God's call to be fruitful is to bear children, which is good and important and creative work. But God's invitation to be fruitful extends far beyond bearing children. It extends to any sphere in which we find ourselves—friendships, activism, work, church life, and so on.

We are called to create. Embedded in our call to create is a relational assumption. God creates relationally as evidenced in the phrase, "Let us" (v. 26; more on the Trinity in chapter 5). God creates people, not a person. God gives the first people a commission that requires both of them. There is a sense that we are united and called to service of one another. This was at the heart of Luther's framing of vocation as the call to lovingly serve one's neighbor. This element of relational service and bondedness should be preserved as we think about God's call for us to create. We don't create simply for the sake of our own ambitions, but for the sake of loving our neighbor. That is part of what makes our work distinctively Christian.

Of course, creating in loving service of each other can take all kinds of shapes. It can look like restoring broken places, people, and systems in a way that brings about renewal and helps illuminate what God is up to. It can look like creating new pathways and solutions, and sometimes new systems, when we sense that the fruit of renewal requires a type of end that ultimately leads toward new beginnings. And sometimes it's creating space—or advocating—for someone's opinion or idea (even if that person is you!).

When we weave this third nesting doll of calling in with the other two, we start to get a picture that we're made to belong to Jesus and to creatively work toward God's mission of redemption in the world. Our identity is found in our belonging to Jesus. Our purpose is to participate in the mission of redemption. Our God-given creativity becomes a vehicle for the first two.

Again, this creativity can play out in any sphere of our lives, including our work. There are so many spaces and moments that God beckons us to lean into our creative selves. It might be a conversation with a friend, cooking dinner for our kids, apologizing to our partner, a solution to a work problem, and more. Chapter 6 will take up creativity in a more robust way.

*We are called to follow Jesus by creatively working, especially toward God's mission of redemption in the world.*

### The Fourth and Outermost Doll: The Call to Particulars

God calls us to particulars—particular people, places, moments, tasks, and roles. Importantly, these particulars flow from what is more central—the call to belong to Jesus, the call to orient our lives toward redemption, and the call to create.

The Bible is rich with stories of God calling people—communities and individuals—to particulars. One of my favorite stories of a particular call is the story of Mary. Mary's story of calling starts when she was visited by an angel and told that she was going to give birth to the Son of God. First of all, I can't even imagine what sweet, young Mary was thinking. Whatever was running through her mind, she responded to the angel that she was a servant of God's and that she would do whatever God wanted her to. She would be faithful to what God called her to (Luke 1:26–38).

Even though that angel visitation feels out of this world, and the virginal conception that follows it is hard to wrap my brain around, I love this story for all the ordinariness that follows.

Jesus grows inside of Mary's womb. If Mary was anything like me when she was pregnant, her feet were swollen and she was always sweating. She was hungry all the time, but never for anything healthy. The bigger Jesus got, the harder it was for her to breathe. She had to take lots of breaks and stay out of the sun.

Eventually, Mary endured the pain of labor and likely fed Jesus from her breast, waking with him every few hours those first few months. She looked after him in the daily, hourly, sometimes momentary ways that parents do. Then as Jesus grew, she bore witness to his walking and talking and playing. It's easy to be drawn to the incredible nature of God's call to Mary. But just as critical is realizing that God's call to her played out in ordinary work. Beyond Mary's willingness with the angel that day, it's the compilation of doing all the ordinary work that fully makes up her response to God. Particular callings often play out in just that—the particulars.

I'm convinced that so much of God's call to the particulars takes place in the eye-level view of life. On the walk to a neighborhood coffee shop, in a conversation with a friend, in the voting booth or the grocery aisle, the movie theater or the gym. Every day we are met with so many opportunities to bear witness to the image of God, the one who seeks to redeem our interactions with people, the shopping decisions we make, and the projects we give our time and money to. Those are the spaces in which we too can acknowledge that we are up for doing whatever God wants us to do.

For most of us, God's callings don't come all at once and don't stay fixed for our entire lives. Plus, the specifics of how our lives work—who we're connected to, where we live, what we do for work—change shape in different seasons. Our lives and our work environments are dynamic, not static. In order to sense the Spirit of God at work, calling us toward particulars, we need to look for manna.

You may remember manna from the Old Testament story in Exodus 16 when God provides food day by day for the Israelites. The story goes that the Israelites were stuck in the desert and wandering and not sure what to do next. They were in an unknown land, everything had changed, and they were unprepared. It's easy to imagine that they too were feeling overwhelmed, anxious, and isolated.

The story takes place in the Desert of Sin (talk about a foreboding name)—a barren place without much food—a stark contrast from Egypt where they had been before. Though they were treated poorly as slaves in Egypt, they found themselves longing for the days when they had "pots of meat and all the food they wanted" (v. 3). They found themselves longing for security. They were frustrated that God had brought them into such a barren place. In the story, God hears their longing and responds to their need by promising manna from heaven each new day.

Manna, a flaky, bland, eatable substance, was a residual by-product of morning dew. God instructed the Israelites to gather one day's worth of manna each morning as they woke up. The only time they were instructed to collect more than a day's worth was in anticipation of the Sabbath—the day of rest. If and when they tried to store up extra manna beyond their daily dose, the manna would spoil and be worthless.

Manna teaches us about the ordinary pace of God's grace. It teaches us that our God is in the day-to-day details. Manna shows us that the grandness of God does indeed show up in small, even bland ways. Manna reveals to us that God's promise of being with us does not always come in the form of an invitation to stand in front of a burning bush like Moses or to parent the Son of God like Mary. More often, God's fulfillment of promises manifests as ongoing provisions that allow us to wake up and to take the next step and take heart that even—maybe especially—in the details, God is leading the way. In this day-by-day approach, manna also teaches us that we can't store up God's grace. If we spend our energy trying to hoard God's provisions out of step with our instructions, they might even spoil.

So as you think about where you are on your journey of calling, think about this: God's mercy is new each morning. The rising sun and the morning dew bring us a new day. The sun sets and the moon makes its way to the sky. And then the sun rises again. A day can hold only so much, and we can travel only so far. Our willingness to depend on the rhythm of God's ordinary grace might very well be the bedrock for how we do the daily work of centering ourselves as we seek to follow Christ in all the particulars of life. In this, we will have great days—days when God's manna tastes sweet. And we will have tough days—days when God's manna tastes especially bland. Most days will be something in between— time spent doing ordinary tasks, going ordinary places, having ordinary conversations with the people we find ourselves with. My prayer is that you are able to delight in the day-by-day, on-the-wayness of life lived in response to our God, who provides for us and guides us.

Putting the nesting dolls together, we get this: *We are called to follow Jesus by creatively working in love for others, especially toward God's mission of redemption in the world, through particular relationships, roles, places, tasks, and moments.*

As we embark on the task of meaningful work, let's look at this phrase as a bit of a north star—a guiding light that remains steady as the entire universe moves around it.

## EXERCISE: Map Your Road of Calling

Materials needed: paper and drawing supplies (I prefer colored markers).

The goal of this exercise is to remember—to recall and visualize—how God has guided you thus far. Block out at least fifteen minutes. Try to find somewhere quiet, or maybe use your headphones.

You are going to draw your road of calling, including significant-to-you milestones along the way—events, seasons, roles, people, and so on—that stand out on your journey thus far. As you start, consider the shape of your road. If there have been many pivots and surprises, maybe your road has a dozen switchbacks. Or if your journey has felt especially difficult, maybe set it on the side of a steep mountain. I've had people tell me that they picture actual roads they know well—the road their childhood house was on or the road they now run on. Really visualize it.

You are going to fill in different milestones along the way. As you do this, think about the nesting dolls of calling and the idea of calling as dynamic. Include your sense of God's call to particulars, but also include when you sensed the call to follow Jesus along the way. Include how things changed and evolved.

With each of your milestones, include visuals that portray what that milestone or season felt like. For example, you might include a sign indicating a roadblock or falling rocks from a nearby mountain to indicate a season when you felt like God was saying no. Or you might draw a group of your friends or a waterfall or a roadside fruit stand to signify a season of harvest. Remember, this is your road; there is no wrong way to do this exercise.

Feel free to share your road with someone else who can help you process it more. And keep it close by as you make your way through the rest of this book.

# PART TWO

# Who Will You Become?

May the road rise up to meet you.

May the wind be always at your back.

May the sun shine warm upon your face,

the rains fall soft upon your fields, and
until we meet again,

may you feel held as you rest in the palm of
God's hand.

Irish Blessing (remixed just a little)

# 4

# Walk the Entrepreneurial Way

After seminary, Dan and I had a string of apartments and eventually a house that each became kind of a gathering place for our friends. We'd get together on breezy Southern California evenings after our shifts as personal trainers, creative directors, adjunct faculty, and government workers. We'd sit around our weathered picnic table with a six-pack and talk about the stuff that mattered most to us. As the sun went down and we switched the market lights on, our conversations were equal parts laughter and tears—equal parts angst and hope. Our friends were like us, people in their late twenties and early thirties early on in their careers. Over time, our ritual became a time to talk about our work.

Our conversations were split between the work we dreamed of doing and the parts about our jobs that made us feel restless or discouraged. We laughed and lamented about how we were all sort of making it up as we went. We talked about how the rules that guided our parents' work felt completely off the table for us. And how that made most parental advice all the more frustrating. Inevitably, each conversation culminated with our deeper wrestling about what we sensed God calling us toward and how far we still felt from getting there.

When I started my doctoral work, these backyard conversations with my friends became the soundtrack for my biggest questions. The stories I heard around that table became the guiding voices that shaped my research agenda. I wanted to know the following: What did it take for people to actually do meaningful work that paid well in this new world? What were the rules, best practices, and hidden secrets for living an integrated life? How might God's big, beautiful, and gritty story serve as a guiding light for the way forward amid so much change?

As I said earlier, I come from a family of teachers and entrepreneurs. My parents are both small-business owners. So from the time I was a kid, my model for work was as an entrepreneur. I learned to pitch an idea to would-be customers before I learned to get a job. I learned to market and do my own accounting before I ever wrote a résumé. And I learned to cultivate listening to my internal hunches about what would sell before I ever learned to ask for a raise.

Somewhat naively, I thought, *In a world where everyone has to figure out so much of work on their own, what if I could somehow integrate my faith values and my entrepreneurial instincts into a process or a method? And what if I could teach other people that method?* Said another way, what if entrepreneurship could be a model for vocational formation—a model for pursuing the ongoing process of being formed in Christ's likeness for the sake of responding to God's callings? And not just for people who wanted to start a business but for any person wanting to faithfully respond to God in our changing world?

So I set out to find anything that could help—practices, principles, data, an existing model—from folks who had started successful businesses and nonprofits and were faithful Christians. I had people nominate entrepreneurs who fit this bill and were motivated by their faith in their work (whether it showed up explicitly or not).

What I eventually discovered is that there are indeed some common characteristics of what it means to be both an entrepreneur and a faithful Christian. And these traits are so wonderfully human that the rest of us can use them as a model for mapping meaningful work in a changing world.

The characteristics came to light in a round of surveys with over fifty entrepreneurs and through more in-depth interviews with ten of the fifty.[1] As I worked to distill these features, I paid special attention to the various rhythms of activities, habits, and spiritual practices of entrepreneurs. Then as I tested the applicability of what I found with over five hundred people in classrooms and cohorts and conversations along the way, certain elements of the model were refined while others were reinforced. By the way, I'm not the first person to discover many of these characteristics. In literature ranging from innovation to faith and work to storytelling and art, the common traits of what I refer to as the entrepreneurial way have been well documented under other labels.

Mostly—as is often the case with life—it was people's stories that revealed the most. So much so that I started asking almost everyone I spent time with some of the same questions I asked my research participants. By far, the most illuminating answers came from the following four questions: How have you learned to define success? How have you learned to define failure? What practices have moved you toward success? What practices have helped you deal with failure?

Listening to people's answers to these questions has helped me to see that though our stories are different, they are also somehow similar. Whether it's an entrepreneur dealing with the highs and lows of starting a new business, an artist trying to make a career out of what they love to do, a senior leader looking for more meaning, or someone having to start over after loss, people tell different stories but with similar themes: heartbreak and hope, overwhelm and optimism, chaos and courage.

As a result of all my research, I've come to believe in what I'll call the *entrepreneurial way*—a way of thinking and acting that is about paying deep attention to the needs of people and creatively joining in God's mission of redemption in the world. Remember the nesting dolls from the previous chapter? I said that a way to think about calling is like a set of nesting dolls: *We are called to follow Jesus by creatively working in love for others, especially toward God's mission of redemption in the world, through particular relationships, roles, places, tasks, and moments.* The entrepreneurial way is a way of working and living that helps us respond faithfully to God's callings.

For some, walking the entrepreneurial way is something that sounds good but is for people who have loads of strategic creativity or want to start a business. Yes, there are those of us who intuitively move through the world as entrepreneurs. But as I've watched hundreds of people experiment with the tools and experience transformation, I'm convinced that the entrepreneurial way is for anyone trying to do meaningful work in a changing world.

I'm convinced that in the face of a changing world, meaning comes to those who have eyes to see and ears to hear. What I mean by this is that meaning comes to those who are willing to engage in holy wrestling. Meaning comes to those who are willing to faithfully and creatively press into the foggy unknown, trusting that our dynamic God is leading the way. Meaning comes to those who are willing to do the complicated inner work of sorting through pain and longing so that we can grow in attunement to the day-by-day graces of God on whatever road we are traveling.

### Getting Our Bearings for the Way Forward

In order to find our bearings for the way forward, I want to pause and talk about where we've been. We've already done a good bit of work that I'd like to think of as *naming the terrain*. We named that the new world of work is demanding and difficult—that it can make us feel overwhelmed, lonely, and anxious (among other things). If it helps to picture an actual map, maybe these feelings show up as rocky, swampy, or desertlike terrain—pick a visual that captures how you experience the changing world of work.

Then we named some of the impacts of larger forces of change such as globalization and accelerated technology. We said that we feel less like we're riding up a smooth escalator and more like we're traversing down white water rapids—without always having the skills to do so. Again, if it helps to visualize these forces of change, perhaps picture rivers that cut through the rocky or desertlike atmospheres you're already imagining.

We also named and unpacked some of the dysfunctional beliefs that permeate thinking on calling, and we set the foundation for a day-by-day, on-the-way theology of calling. It might help to visualize these messages as road signs on your map—places where there's a fork in the road or a detour, or a sign that says you're 137 miles from your destination.

Now we need roads. There are, of course, the well-worn paths to work that previous generations used. Why not just try to build on these or adapt them for our changing world? Sometimes this strategy works, but much of the time it doesn't. The old roads that worked so well on a different map oftentimes don't carry over as viable pathways in the uncharted world we're in.

It's here that I want to suggest the entrepreneurial way as a model for traversing, pathfinding, and ultimately creating roads for the way forward in this new world of work. The entrepreneurial way in its simplest form captures how entrepreneurs think and act. And as I said earlier, it's a way of thinking and acting that is about paying deep attention to the needs of people and creatively joining in God's mission of redemption in the world. The word *way* is important as it reminds us that we live life in motion. We're all on a journey from some sort of point *a* to point *z*.

Here are our ground rules for the entrepreneurial way—the framework for our map to meaningful work:

- *Our north star*: We are called to follow Jesus by creatively working in love for others, especially toward God's mission of redemption in the world, through particular relationships, roles, places, tasks, and moments.
- *Our road trip mantra*: Seize Opportunity. Create Value. Face Risk. We expect this to be a lifelong journey. Along the way, we will learn to notice and pursue opportunity so that we may create value, even and especially in the face of risk (see the next section).
- *How we will behave along the way*: We'll be rooted in relationships, trust that we're creative, and build resilience.
- *What we will spend our time doing*: We will empathize with our neighbors. We will imagine, What if? We will take the next doable risks. And we will make space to reflect with gratitude on all that God has done.

Each of these bullet points deserves significant attention. We took up our north star in chapter 3, which was about calling. In this chapter, I'll focus on our road trip mantra. Chapters 5, 6, and 7 are devoted to how we will behave. And chapters 8 through 11 take up what we will spend our time doing.

## Our Road Trip Mantra

Seize Opportunity. Create Value. Face Risk.

Recently, I was chatting with Jason. He was a few years into resurrecting a nonprofit that had nearly fizzled out under previous leadership. When he assumed leadership, it had run out of money, was unclear on its mission, and had major personnel problems. As we talked, Jason explained to me that although he hadn't started the organization, he sort of felt like an entrepreneur because resurrecting the place had required reorienting the mission around new needs and cobbling together a financial runway for the organization to get back on its feet. As he was processing, Jason turned to me and asked, "Do you think I'm an entrepreneur?"

"Well, what do you think?" I responded.

He said, "I feel like an entrepreneur even though I haven't started a business."

Jason and I talked about how the word *entrepreneur* is sometimes more harmful than it is helpful. In my experience, it is one of those words that people either wholeheartedly identify with or completely reject for themselves. The same can be said about the words *leader* and *creative*. Because society centers particular types of leaders or entrepreneurs, our collective imaginations can be too narrow. If we don't picture ourselves as the leader of a giant organization or the founder of a thriving tech start-up, we might doubt that these frameworks apply to us. In my experience, no one is served well by these insider-outsider dynamics. Not you, not others, not the mission of God in the world.

So opt in or opt out if you like. But my bias is that no one type of person has the claim on what it means to be a creative, a leader, or an entrepreneur. Everyone is creative. Everyone has opportunities to lead in some way or another. All of us can walk the entrepreneurial way. Whether you are in a nine-to-five job with benefits, starting a side hustle, or on a job hunt and up against more experienced professionals or more tech-savvy individuals, we can all notice and seize opportunity, create value, and bravely face risk.

### Seize Opportunity

At the core of what it means to walk the entrepreneurial way is to seize opportunity. I wrote much of this book in the middle of the COVID-19 quarantine. In those early days of intense lockdown, one of my favorite quarantine errands was to go to our local cheese shop. Early in the pandemic, do you know what the cheese folks were selling? Toilet paper! Why? Because where I live in California, toilet paper was impossible to find. So the cheese shop seized an opportunity. They knew that if they offered something that was in high demand, they would be able to not only generate badly needed revenue but also drive traffic into the store to buy cheese.

Noticing opportunity and actually pursuing it are two different things. We've already said that noticing opportunity—especially in the midst of change—takes eyes to see and ears to hear. It takes a willingness to simultaneously grieve what was and hope for what might be. It takes both a posture of reflection and a bias toward action. Plus, in a changing world, we cannot calm our fears with neat and tidy answers. The world is unpredictable, nonlinear, disruptive, and chaotic. Remember the concept lean in and let go (chapter 2)? It's the idea that in the midst of change, the goal isn't to grab for control but rather to let go.

Embedded in the entrepreneurial way are certain dispositions that help combat our fears and enable us to lean in and let go for the sake of noticing and seizing opportunity.

I like to think of these dispositions kind of like muscles. When I was first trying to identify these muscles, I combed the literature on entrepreneurship looking for patterns of identity because I wanted to ground my research on practices within a larger framework of identity. What I wanted to know is, What is at the core of the people who could notice and pursue opportunity in a changing world? I didn't know exactly what to expect. I suspected there was a set of soft skills or qualities that entrepreneurs shared. But I didn't know what they'd be or if there would be explicit links to the Christian story.

What I discovered is so encouraging. I found that core to the identity of successful and faithful entrepreneurs are three dispositions: *creative*, *resilient*, and *relational*. Both in the literature and then as I conducted my research, these muscles presented themselves in the stories of so many of the people I spoke with.

Creative, resilient, and relational: what I love about this list is how wholeheartedly Christian it feels to me. Creativity? Well, that's our first story about God. Resilience? That's our climactic story in Christ. Relational? That's the church. The coherence between the entrepreneurial way and the big story of our faith is such good news! It means that as people who bear the image of God, we are in our essence creative, resilient, and relational beings and we indeed have what it takes to create paths toward meaningful work in a changing world. Each of these muscles is so important that we'll explore them further in the next three chapters. Here, let me just offer that these three deeply human capacities are the foundation for noticing and seizing opportunity in our work.

### Create Value

The entrepreneurial way says that when we pursue opportunity we do so with the intention of creating value. But value is in the eye of the beholder. Embedded in the fabric of our society are many, many ways humans measure value. If a project we undertake makes money, we might say it has financial value. If it strengthens relationships, we might say it has relational value. If it contributes positively to the social well-being of a community, we might say it has social value. So we must ask ourselves, What type of value are we supposed to work toward as Christians?

To answer this, let's turn our eyes to our road trip north star: we are called to follow Jesus by creatively working in love for others, especially toward God's mission of redemption in the world, through particular relationships, roles, places, tasks, and moments. This means that we can create value through our work in alignment with God's call to be a people creatively working toward redemption in the world. We create value through the particular relationships, roles, places, tasks, and moments God beckons us toward.

When I use the word *value*, I'm not talking about our value as people. I'm not equating the works we do with what God thinks of us. Our value as beloved children of God doesn't depend on whether we create value for the rest of the world through our work. But our work is an invitation to express our value to the world—to reflect that we bear the image of God and therefore all that we put our hearts and minds to are calibrated toward God's north star of redemption.

What does it actually look like for our day-by-day work to be calibrated toward redemption? I'll admit that redemption can feel like a big, audacious, and glorious goal that is just abstract enough to make it hard to measure or know when we're making progress. Plus, it would be arrogant to assume that as individuals we can redeem what feels broken. We trust that God is the source of redemption, and while we're called to participate in it, God doesn't always make all things new right before our eyes or even in ways we've come to expect or hope for. Sometimes we join God as seed planters or crop cultivators or harvest laborers. There is always a bigger picture beyond what we can see, which can make the idea of redemption feel fuzzy.

The Bible has a lot to say about redemption. From God's relationship to Israel to the new covenant established through Jesus, God is interested in redeeming and restoring what is broken or distant from God. In a sense, we can look around and notice anything—relationships, systems, people—and assume that God desires redemption.

In terms of spotting what redemption actually looks like, the concept of bearing fruit helps me to wrap my mind around it. Throughout Scripture, we have examples of God's goodness bearing fruit—whether it's the fruit in the garden of Eden, the images of Jesus as a vine, the fruit of true prophets, or the fruit of the Holy Spirit. So what are the fruits of redemption? And can that fruit help us to know both where God is at work and what to work toward ourselves? I'm sure some of us can come up with a long list of the fruits of redemption. In fact, if this is the way your brain works, I encourage you to do this with others in your life.

Here, let me suggest justice and shalom as fruits of redemption. Amy Sherman, author of the seminal book *Kingdom Calling: Vocational Stewardship for the Common Good*, offers helpful frameworks for how justice and shalom are related to our work and God's callings for us. Therefore, I'll draw closely from her work in this section. Though she wouldn't use the phrase *fruits of redemption*, her thorough exegesis around these concepts offers a multifaceted picture that can help us move past the fuzziness of what redemption looks like.

Sherman roots many of her teachings on vocation around the biblical idea of righteousness. She would say (and I would agree) that being righteous people is at the heart of what it means to faithfully live out our lives in response to God. Righteous people are those who view their own flourishing as a means to bless others. Flourishing for the sake of others stands in contrast to those who put their own economic, social, and personal needs ahead of the needs of their community.[2]

Part of what it means to be righteous is to *do justice and pursue shalom wherever you are*. So what exactly are justice and shalom? The Bible has a lot to say about both of these concepts. First, throughout Scripture and especially the Old Testament, we see justice as central to the identity of God and God's relationship with Israel. God is one who judges, paying special attention to give justice to the weak and the orphan and to uphold the dignity and rights of people who are suffering or who don't have access to the benefits of high society (Ps. 82).

Sherman says that justice has a three-dimensional quality consisting of rescue, equity, and restoration.[3] The work of rescue is about challenging the worst types of injustice, such as the wicked hunting down the weak (Ps. 10),[4] the acquittal of the guilty at the cost of the innocent (Isa. 5:23), and the swift shedding of innocent blood (Isa. 59:7).[5] Equity is about working with fairness to ensure "that the poor and weak are not disproportionately burdened by society's common problems."[6] Scripture describes the righteous king who will righteously judge the poor (Isa. 11:4) and do what is right in the land (Jer. 23:5).

Restoration captures the relational element of biblical justice. Sherman argues that biblical justice is not "solely concerned with the punishment of wrongdoing, but with the healing of wrongdoers and their restoration to the community."[7] Sherman offers Zechariah 8:16–17 as a preview of restoration. God meets the Israelites, who are full of unjust offense against God, with both a punishment and a corrective, a promise of both forgiveness and restoration of relationship.[8]

Biblical shalom is another way to capture peaceful wholeness in God's kingdom, which means that shalom is squarely in contrast to oppression and injustice.[9] Just as righteous people do justice, the community ought to be a place where shalom is present. Sherman talks about shalom—or peaceful wholeness—across four relational spheres: peace with God, peace with self, peace with others, and peace with the creation. Increasing peace and wholeness in any of these areas is an expression of shalom.

First, peace with God is at the core of God's plan for redemption. Peace with God happens through both intimacy with God and appreciation of and engagement with beauty in the world, including God's people.[10] Second, peace with self is marked by health/wholeness of our bodies (Isa. 32:3–4; 35:6; 65:19), hope in what is to come (Pss. 68:6; 113:9; Isa. 42:3–4), and comfort for the wounded in spirit (Isa. 54).[11]

Author and spiritual formation expert Ruth Haley Barton argues that peace with self is marked in part by one's ability to pay attention, especially to one's questions.[12] Third, peace with others includes deep unity with other people (Isa. 25:6–9; Rev. 7:9–20) as well as shalom.[13] Deeper unity with other people is a fruit of our labors of justice. Peace with others includes a lack of violence. Finally, Sherman argues that peace with creation manifests as economic flourishing for all people (Isa. 49:10; 65:21–22; Joel 3:18; Mic. 4:4) and sustainability of natural resources (Isa. 35:1–2, 7).[14] This economic flourishing and natural sustainability happen when believers commit themselves to alleviate suffering and find new ways to participate in the ongoing breaking in of God's kingdom.[15]

Okay, that's a lot to take in. How do the fruits of justice and shalom show up in the world? What kinds of things might we point to in order to both name and cultivate these fruits of redemption in our contexts and communities?

Justice and shalom can take many different shapes—from the decisions and processes that feel life altering to the small daily moments that help us remember we are indeed a day-by-day, on-the-way people. Sometimes these fruits show up when we actively work against powers that harm the innocent—systems that exploit the work of children or migrant workers. Justice might look like writing new anti-discrimination policies in our workplaces or in our governments. Or shalom might be present when we slow down long enough to truly listen to a person in need or celebrate the accomplishment of another. Justice and shalom might look like a choice to print materials on recycled paper or to carpool to work to save on fuel emissions. Still other times, justice might look like apologizing to or forgiving someone with whom we live or work. The fruits of redemption are indeed alive and well wherever there are people putting the needs of the community front and center.

### *Face Risk*

Pursuing opportunity to create value almost always comes in the face of risk. *Facing risk* is an active posture. Even the slanted nature of the italic script represents that entrepreneurs have to *lean into* risk. Is risk scary? Yes, it certainly can be. Does risk end in failure? Sometimes. Is the opportunity to create value in the face of risk worth the potential failure? Mostly, yes.

Facing risk requires a steadiness and a confidence that come from within us and also from a sense that it's not all about us. Tom and David Kelley, the brothers behind the leading design firm IDEO, have been formative to my thinking about what it takes to face risk. They make a compelling argument that everyone has creative capacity but that many of us are held back from fulfilling our creative potential because we're conditioned to lack creative confidence.[16] In other words, we lack the confidence to face risk. Unfortunately, prevailing broken systems, toxic relationships, and deeply held societal values breed in us four fears that the Kelley brothers say get in the way of creativity: fear of the unknown, fear of being judged, fear of taking the first step, and fear of losing control.[17] In a word, we know deep down that failure is often accompanied by shame.

*New York Times* bestselling author and research professor Brené Brown has done groundbreaking research on the topic of shame. She writes, "Shame derives its power from being unspeakable. . . . If we speak shame, it begins to wither. Just the way exposure to light was deadly for the gremlins, language and story bring light to shame and destroy it."[18] Brown argues that in American culture, we have lost our capacity to hold pain. This is because we live in a culture that equates vulnerability with weakness, and we have decided that weakness is disgusting.[19]

So much of our capacity to face risk—so that we might seize opportunity and create value—is rooted in what we think about failure. If we fear failure, risk is scary. If we are comfortable with failure, risk feels more doable. Chapter 7 is about building resilience—a muscle that enables us to embrace setback and change and therefore take more risks. Chapter 10 is about risk-taking as a practice for the way forward. So we'll spend plenty of time in the rest of the book on risk. Here, let me just state that if risk is something you're uncomfortable with, that's okay. It's a muscle that can be built up. But in order to do so, we have to face what makes us afraid—what steals our creative confidence. Whether it's the shame we feel or even trauma from past failures or the fear of the messy unknown, we've got to get really honest about where we are so that we can press into where we want to go.

## EXERCISE: Calibrating Success and Failure

Consider the Road of Calling exercise from the previous chapter. Or, if you haven't done it yet, think back over your career and life thus far. With that in mind, journal your answers to the following questions:

1. How have you learned to define success?
2. How have you learned to define failure?
3. What practices have moved you toward success?
4. What practices have helped you deal with failure?

# Be Rooted in Relationships

I grew up mowing my grandma's lawn. When she moved in across the street from us, she was too old to push the mower. I was just old enough. So every week when the grass was green, I'd make my way to her place. Her yard was small, so the job was quick. Except for the big hill at the back, which always took some finesse. Just as I was wrestling with the automatic mower going downhill, my grandma would pop her head out the back door and holler, "Stop inside when you're done!"

That's because she mostly paid me in food and stories. I realize now, it was the best business arrangement I ever had. I'd sit at the kitchen table and listen to her talk about her life as a young woman. Mostly she talked about Eddie and dancing. Eddie was the reckless love she had before she settled down with my grandpa. And dancing—dancing was the thing she did late into the night with her sisters to take refuge from how hard life was in the Great Depression.

But she also talked to me about her work—her time in business school, her office jobs, her bosses, and how she started a bookkeeping business out of her house once she had kids. She loved her kids—all nine of them. But I got to see how much she loved them and how much they loved her all the time. At that kitchen table dipping cookies in milk, when it was just the two of us, I learned just how much she loved her career.

From an early age, my grandma helped me know what it looked and sounded like when someone was proud of their work. Her stories were part of what made me want my own work to matter. Her brilliance—which I've only come to understand decades later—is that she was helping me to be proud of my mowing job too. She was teaching me that it was good and fruitful—and that it mattered.

The rhythm and quality of relationships in our lives become the well that we draw from in success and failure alike. For better or worse, people shape us. They love us and they hurt us. They inspire us and they discourage us. They cheer us on and they fail our expectations. And to this holy dance of friendship—even with its flaws—we are drawn. God beckons us to draw near to others in the weary and wild and winsome moments of our life and work.

The idea that people are central to our vocational formation was certainly true for the entrepreneurs in my study. I asked them about the sources that had helped them the most in the starting and running of their businesses and in their ability to integrate their faith into their work. Their top responses were about other people: mentors, other entrepreneurs, a spiritual leader, and small groups or churches. These were the sources that had contributed the most to who they were and the journey they'd taken.

Relationships were central to how they defined success and failure, central to their sense of professional and personal formation, and central to the day-to-day ways they carry out their work. Every time I talk to an entrepreneur about what has made them successful, they tell me about the people in their lives—from partners in marriage to family members, neighbors, small groups, and business partners alike—and about how these relationships have taught them and helped them along the way.

## Defining Success

Remember, I asked folks in the in-depth round of interviews four specific questions: How have you learned to define success? How have you learned to define failure? What practices have moved you toward success? What practices have helped you deal with failure? And since that initial round of data collection, I have asked this same set of questions to up-and-coming leaders, seasoned professionals, and stay-at-home parents alike. In the answers they gave to the first four questions, there was a common theme: a positive impact on people.

This set of questions reveals a bias that snuck into my research. Bias is nearly unavoidable and therefore important to name. My bias is that we are always learning, always growing, always changing. So when I ask people about success, I don't ask, "What is success?" or "How do you define success?" No, I intentionally ask, "How have you *learned* to define success?"

When I ask it this way, people's answers almost always have a resounding theme: part of how they've learned to define success (and subsequently failure) has a lot to do with their impact on other people and other people's impact on them. That's not to say that people aren't aware of and focused on financial success. In fact, one of the first things people will do is offer a caveat about hitting financial goals and the bottom line. But then they settle into what seems to matter most to them—impact on people.

Andrew Laffoon is the founder of Mixbook, a photo book company. When I asked Andrew how he had learned to define success, he talked with me about impact on people in two ways: impact of their product on customers' lives and Mixbook employee flourishing.

Sometimes, after a customer finishes making a photo book or a gift, they write to the team at Mixbook. These notes mean a lot to Andrew. He reflected, "They'd write in to us and say, 'My dad passed away last year and I was struggling to figure out what to do. I really wanted to do something to honor his life, and so I decided to make a photo book, a Mixbook.'"[1] It seemed that the photo book had become a tool for grief and processing—something Andrew hadn't expected when he first started. Through those notes, Andrew and his team heard just how deeply the product they worked on was impacting their customers.

These stories were what helped sustain Andrew as he hit the natural bumps of a start-up along the way. He said, "Whoa! I had no idea how powerful this would be and that is what keeps me going, because what I realize is I'd rather do *that* and *that* be the thing, because *that* actually makes an impact on the world."[2] Knowing that Mixbook was not only a photo book but also a tool that gave people important space became a measure of success for Andrew.

The second part of Andrew's definition of success was related to the flourishing of his employees. He described how this was something he had come to learn the hard way. In the beginning, he told me his mantra was more like, "You just hire great people and hopefully you don't have to fire anybody. They just do great work for you."[3] Over time, it became clear that simply picking great people and hoping for the best wasn't a sustainable strategy. Andrew said, "No, everybody needs feedback. Everybody needs help growing, and we should build an environment where people can do their best work and grow faster than they're going to grow anywhere else and position them for the next job that they're going to take."[4]

It's encouraging that Andrew worked so intentionally to cultivate flourishing—to enable people to do their best work and grow fast. But what I am even more encouraged about is that Andrew's definition of success was in fact learned—and likely evolving even since our conversation. He did not know that his product was going to be a tool for grief and that this would matter so much to him it would become a measure of success. He did not know how much he would have to focus on helping employees flourish—yet that had become important enough to be a measure of success. In this way, the customers and the employees actually formed Andrew's definition of success.

Consider how the people you've worked alongside and/or served have impacted and formed your definition of success.

Maybe a former colleague modeled for you how to speak truth to power, and that's now part of what you imagine success to look like. Maybe your dad worked as a doctor, and so caring for the sick or healing people (even if it's not through medicine) is part of how you've learned to define success. Maybe someone who works for you is excellent in conflict. And so you've come to define success partly by your capacity to usher in peace in the workplace. Now consider how you might answer the question, How have you learned to define success? How does positive impact on people show up?

Relationships sustain us and embolden us. They help us and they hold us. Relationships are central to our formation. I believe the reason they're so central has a lot to do with the way we're designed.

## Designed for Relationship

We're made in the image of a relational God. Our basis for this starts in Genesis—in the same place we see evidence of God's call to create and that God is a worker. In the poetic ode to God as Creator that is Genesis 1, we read that God has created humankind in the image of God. God says, "Let *us* make humankind in *our* image" (v. 26, emphasis added).

Who in the world is *us*? It's honestly hard to know what the ancient Israelites would have meant by this plurality. But one commonly accepted interpretation is to understand this verse through the lens of the Christian doctrine of the Trinity. If you're like me, the theological concept of the Trinity is a complicated concept to grasp. Three in one. One in three. What does that mean? I want to parse the Trinity just a bit

116

as I believe it's foundational for understanding why relationships are so powerful in our lives.

The Trinity consists of God the Creator, Jesus, and the Holy Spirit. Some people talk about these three entities as God the Father, God the Son, and God the Spirit. That's fine too. Though I might even switch back and forth, I think it's helpful whenever possible to view God beyond the lens of human gender. God the Creator, Jesus, and the Holy Spirit are each distinctive yet unified in eternal communion. That's a loaded phrase—each distinctive yet unified in eternal communion.

*Distinctive* means that we see evidence of each part of the Trinity having its own distinct presence in the kingdom of God. *Eternal* means forever. *Communion* is a way to describe sharing intimate space with God. So if the members of the Trinity are distinct, yet united in eternal communion, then they are each their own entity, yet forever united and sharing close, intimate space with one another.

It's this unified yet distinct nature of God that undergirds our own relational makeup. The fact that we're designed to image a relational God sets the stage for the profound relational invitation we have in Christ. In Christ, we are welcomed into relationship with the Triune God. This invitation in Christ becomes the vehicle for our own communion with God and subsequently our relationship with others. We are wired for relationship. It's why other people impact us so much. And it's why we have such capacity to impact others.

Being made in the image of a relational God is not just a characteristic; it's a commission! Being in relationship is a prerequisite to spreading the love of God that we receive to our neighbors. This is how we spread good news. It's central to how we are to walk in the way of Jesus.

Here, I want to name two very specific ways relationships can help us along this journey of calling, especially as we're seeking to think about how our faith and our work illuminate one another. Relationships help us *close the gap*, and relationships *catalyze creativity*.

### Relationships Help Us Close the Gap

We've talked before about vocational formation—the ongoing process of being formed for God's callings. Part of *how* vocational formation happens is through the people we work and live alongside. At the heart of God's work in us is an invitation to close the gap between who we are and who we're continually called to become.

This was certainly true for both Andrew and Sarah (whom you'll meet in chapter 6). In both of their cases, the people they worked for and the customers they served impacted their evolving definitions of success. In addition to this, relationships help how we listen, make key choices, and react when things get tough.

Uli Chi is the cofounder of Computer Human Interaction, a company that pioneered 3D modeling software for customer user experience. He is an accomplished entrepreneur and a respected leader. When I talked with Uli about what had helped him move toward his definition of success, he described how a small group of Christian business owners helped him at key milestones in his work. This group met regularly to talk through the struggles of owning and running a business, including the work of discerning what God wanted them to do.[5] As we talked, I was struck by Uli's description of how this group had helped form his character toward the call of God over time. To use the language of this book, Uli's group helped him to listen and to walk the entrepreneurial way day by day in a manner that helped him to follow the lead of the Spirit in the dance that is life.

Alex Lim is the cofounder of Five Two Foundation, an online fundraising platform for nonprofits. When we talked, I was really struck by Alex's willingness to talk about the hardest parts of his professional life. He had a clear understanding about the ups and downs of what starting and sustaining Five Two had cost him. When I asked him to help me imagine how God had sustained him through the toughest parts, he credited his perseverance to his relationship with his business partner.

Alex talked freely about the fact that he and his business partner had weathered storms together—that they'd had bad days, even what felt like failures together. But Alex said those things didn't make him feel weary in the way he imagined they might have if he hadn't had a partner. He told me that weathering the hard stuff alone would have probably been unbearable. He guessed that without partnership, he likely would have quit a long time ago.[6]

Relationships help us close the gap between who we are and who we're called to be. They help us listen in such a way that we see the manna God provides. The best relationships help us embody our faith in action and encourage us to continually move toward others as a central part of who we are becoming. All the most important things I've learned about my work—and about God and the world and myself for that matter—have come because others have helped me listen to God and grow in my own knowledge and faithfulness.

Reflect on the relationships that have helped you hear what you didn't want to hear or widened your imagination about what's possible. Consider who has helped you believe things you couldn't quite see. And most of all, remember who has helped you to know that even when things get really, really tough, you are held in the palm of God's hand.

## Relationships Catalyze Creativity

Relationships catalyze creativity. In fact, I will go as far as to say that no one person really ever creates alone. Everything we do is part of a larger tapestry of human activity—even if only indirectly.

In his seminal book *Culture Making: Recovering Our Creative Calling*, author and theologian Andy Crouch argues that much of creativity actually happens in relatively small groups. Reflecting on the concentric circles of Jesus's disciples portrayed in the Bible, Crouch notes that culture making is done in groups. He focuses especially on the biblical examples of groups of three, twelve, and seventy.[7] He suggests that today we might prioritize finding a relatively small and intimate group in which to practice creativity.[8] His position is that however complex and daunting a context's challenges are, creativity will almost always come from a relatively small and intimate group of people.[9]

One example of how a relatively small group of people can catalyze creativity is Pixar's Braintrust. I first learned about the Braintrust by reading Ed Catmull's book *Creativity, Inc.* In that book, Catmull describes that the Braintrust exists to help identify and solve problems for upcoming Pixar movies by giving feedback and ideating to move projects forward. It is almost as if the Pixar Braintrust supports a story and its tellers through a metamorphic-like process of creativity that moves from inception to chaos to finished product, the films we actually see.[10]

The Braintrust started organically among five early members of Pixar working on the *Toy Story* movie as a way to discuss, dissect, and move forward with choices related to the film. Now, twenty-five years later, the Braintrust still gathers every few months to watch reels and examine projects. The group gathers over lunch, and the director/producer explains the state of the project. The people gathered around the table have at least one thing in common: a strong knack for storytelling. They dialogue—often rather emphatically—about what worked and what did not work in the film on the dissection table. Comments, feedback, and frank talk are directed at the story as opposed to the director, writer, or producers.

The Braintrust demonstrates willingness to innovate in that it has a purpose, shared values, and rules of engagement. The Braintrust's *purpose* is to make their films better. Catmull says that in the beginning, all Pixar films "suck." It is up to the men and women at Pixar to "make them unsuck."[11] So in the rawest sense, the Braintrust just helps films to unsuck. There is a set of *shared values* at Pixar and within the Braintrust. The group values story, animation, cutting-edge technology, the truth, and people. In addition to having a purpose and a set of shared values, the Braintrust has established *rules of engagement* in both the ways a group thinks and the way it acts.

Catmull explains that this group works so well in part because of Pixar's communal values of trust and candor. The people in the room are fully committed to the community and the story. Rooted in these commitments, participants have learned that trust and candor are the best way to catalyze creativity among one another. I find these two values especially helpful—actual principles we can look to cultivate in our own relationships.

Over the years, I have gathered a Braintrust for various reasons—different creative projects, strategic direction at work, and my own career. Each time, I have heard from the group things I would not have thought of by myself. Each time, I have ended up making choices that I wouldn't have otherwise.

## EXERCISE: Identify Your Braintrust

Consider forming a Braintrust for your career.

1. Start by thinking about who is already with you on your way, wherever you are in your journey, so you can maximize the people who are already rooting for you. Who are the people you already talk to about your calling and career? Are they coworkers, friends, or partners? Imagine them.

2. As you imagine how you might maximize any latent creativity that exists in these relationships, start by asking the following questions: Do I trust these people? Are they honest with me? Do they embody

their own creative confidence? Are they walking through the world as empathetic neighbors? If you answered yes (even to only some of the questions about some of the people you imagined), you likely have relationships in your own life that can catalyze creativity. You likely have the start of a Braintrust.

3. Try gathering these people as a group to help you workshop something related to your career or calling. Maybe you've been thinking about a job transition. Or maybe you've got an idea for a side hustle or new business. Invite people to help make what you're thinking about or working on better.

Think about these people as the ones who would be willing to pick you up when you stumble along the way. Share with them how you've failed or were beaten down by unfavorable circumstances. Let them know you're thinking of them in this way. Make it a point to seek their advice about the shape your story is taking, and thank them for it. Leaning into your existing relationships with your empathetic neighbors will help you catalyze your own creativity. They will help you identify and actualize the good stuff that has been there all along because God made you creative and gave you the means of relationship.

# 6

# Trust Your Creativity

I hadn't seen Molly in years. She's the childhood best friend of one of my friends from graduate school. When we see each other, it's usually because we're celebrating our mutual friend, Angela, for a birthday, a wedding, or, that day, a graduation.

Molly exudes power. She's the kind of woman that people call boss lady or hashtag for #goals. She's the founder and CEO of a booming fitness company, Girls Gone Strong, which does its part to change the world—one strong woman at a time. I've always experienced Molly as one of the strong women she seeks to build up. Part of what's always caused me to admire her so much is that she has built a meaningful and successful business that impacts the lives of people every day, and I know firsthand how hard that is to do.

So there we were, catching up over pizza and beer. I was telling her a bit about what Dan and I were up to with Long

Winter Media, and she said something I've heard in one way or another from many people since. She said something to the effect of "That's so cool that you can do all of that creative stuff. I'm just not a very creative person."

My mouth fell open. Here was Molly, a woman who had built a business that employed dozens of people, had been featured on all sorts of impressive news outlets, and had impacted the health and mental well-being of so many women. Yet because of the limited ways society uses the word *creativity*, she had opted out of that label.

The reason I was able to recognize the disconnect between how Molly saw herself and how I saw her is because I had been in that exact same spot before. I too had doubted that I was creative. When I started Long Winter, I spent years talking about Dan as the creative half and me as the business half. But the longer we were in business, the more I realized how untrue that was. Sure, Dan's creativity took the form of artistry and storytelling, but mine took the shape of creative strategy and creativity in how I managed clients and artists. And eventually my creativity came to life as a storyteller.

I'm married to an artist, so I know firsthand the special wavelength they live on and the beauty that pours from their soul into the world. I've witnessed what it takes to create art that speaks prophetically to the collective imagination of the world. Artists truly are a unique and precious mirror of God's creative nature in the world.

But creativity is not an attribute reserved for artists. Creativity is about bridging the gap between reality and possibility. In its most basic form, creativity is the ability to generate new and useful ideas. I find comfort in the broadness of "new and useful ideas." Yes, this definition certainly holds space for tech teams, artists, and business owners. But it also holds space for much more ordinary expressions of our identity. Anytime we create something of value—and I mean value in the most expansive and inclusive sense—we exude creativity. I've come to believe that creativity is within us all. I've also come to believe that for an entire set of reasons—some of which I'll get into shortly—we bury our creativity and shield it from the world. The more we do so, the harder it can be to name, access, and exercise it. In my quest to understand creativity in its primal form, I've found myself drawn to an interesting place—playtime with my children.

When my daughter was just learning to walk, she would push a toy shopping cart around our house. She toddled behind the toy with glee until she tried to take it from the living room to the kitchen, where there was a small lip on the floor that halted her abruptly in her tracks. The first several times her cart hit the bump, she cried. To console her, I'd go over, lift the cart over the lip, and she'd be on her way again. And then one time I realized that in lifting the cart up for her, I was stopping her from tapping into her own creative problem-solving abilities. The next time she cried, I did not run to fix the issue. Instead, I told her that she could figure it out and that I'd be there to cheer her on. She immediately tried to mimic how I had picked up the cart, but she wasn't strong enough. There were more tears. I assured her again that she'd figure out another way. After a while, she decided to put her little hands around one of the front wheels and guide it over the lip. She wasn't able to pick up the whole cart, but she could pick up one wheel. It worked! As she realized her success, she looked at me. Beaming with pride at her new discovery, which had proven to be quite useful, she smiled. I looked her in the eyes and said something that I've since repeated many, many times: "You are made to be creative, and this means you've got the tools to do hard things."

My assuredness that she indeed had what it took came from my faith in the creation story. It's encouraging that the very first story we have about God and humans is one rooted in creativity. Genesis helps us imagine that when humans were made we were done so in the image of God. And because we're made in the image of God, who just created the world in the grandest of fashions, our imaginations about what we can do should be inspiring in turn.

Right from the start, our identity is rooted in our belonging to a creative God. If we belong to God and are created in God's creative image, then it's actually quite ordinary to be creative. But it's quite extraordinary that our belonging to God makes this extravagant ability so normal.

Right after God created humans, God gave humans some direction. Genesis 1:28 says, "God blessed them, and God said to them, 'Be fruitful and multiply, and fill the earth and subdue it; and have dominion over the fish of the sea and over the birds of the air and over every living thing that moves upon the earth.'" This verse is often interpreted by theologians as God's creative mandate—God's twofold call to humans to participate in the world creatively and to exercise caring leadership over God's other created beings. In this mandate—this direction from God—we learn that our identity as creative beings is not just for some of us, some of the time. No, being creative is for all of us, all of the time. This creative mandate is God's call to humans. This calling wasn't just while in the garden. It's a calling to humans throughout the ages.

Somewhere along the way, after this expansive and inspiring scene about the God-given creativity inherent in humanity, creativity became incidental instead of central, reserved for the artists and inventors in society. I'm not entirely sure why this happened. Perhaps we see in artists and inventors something that feels especially creative. Perhaps a baby getting her toy from one room to another feels too simple to be part of God's creative calling. Or perhaps, in light of a messy and broken world, our lives feel just a bit more manageable if we're not responsible for creatively addressing the pain in the world.

But if we read the creation narrative closely, it's hard to reject the implications of creativity for our day-to-day lives. If we're made bearing the image of a creative God, this means we've got the hardwiring to apply our creativity toward work that matters. We've got the hardwiring to seize opportunity, join in redemption, and face risk with resolve in our ability to find creative solutions.

The indwelling Spirit of God animates all of creation and human creativity with living breath. This means that whether Molly is building her business or my daughter is problem-solving with her toys, whether we're writing a poem or creatively loving our neighbor, we can trust and draw inspiration from our Creator as we exercise our own creativity in our work and world.

## A Framework for Creativity

Sarah Contrucci Smith is the founder of a global home goods company. Before starting Marra Home, she worked in marketing and got a master's in international development.

Sarah also spent time working with and for businesses that measured their value by both financial and social means. When we talked, she described working with organizations that did skills training and/or distributed small handicrafts as a way to boost local economies around the globe. She saw tons of value in this model of work, but she also wondered if there was room for a different kind of model—one that was built on harvesting local expertise rather than teaching people new skills.[1]

As Sarah started to imagine this new model, she went on a backpacking trip to Central America where she met dozens of artisans who were already producing home goods—pillows, blankets, and other textiles. Sarah learned that the designs these artisans used had been handed down in their communities for hundreds of years. She also learned that because of a dried-up tourist economy, the artisans were increasingly unable to sell their creations, and thus the long-standing designs and techniques were at risk of extinction. Because the finished goods were selling for so little money—or not at all—the children in the community showed little interest in learning the techniques from the elders in the community.

As Sarah met different folks, she pitched them her idea of leveraging the skills they already had. Her idea was to work in collaboration to slightly modify certain elements of the finished product—mostly color palette—and leverage her own marketing skills to position the textiles in an international market. As she reflected with me, Sarah said that she had expected the artisans to say no. She was sensitive to the possibility that her suggestion to change up the colors might violate long-standing traditions and had no interest in doing anything offensive. To her pleasant surprise, the artists were very open to modifying the color palette. They were excited to team up with someone who had Sarah's complementary skills and business credentials and who could potentially open them up to new markets and restore the centrality of their artisan work back into the fabric of their community.

Today, Marra Home is a thriving home goods company that works with six different groups of artisans across Latin America. I want to suggest that embedded in the story of this company are three interrelated elements: *participation*, *anticipation*, and *collaboration*. As I discuss each one, I'll use Sarah's story like a case study to highlight where each of the elements shows up.

### Participation

Human creativity is an act of *participation*—participation in God's creative and redemptive work in this world. No natural wonder, animal, or human has come to exist outside of the creative capacity of God.

We've already learned that in the great scheme of the cosmos, God created people to bear the image of God. In part, this means that we've got the capacity to create.

You don't have to look far to catch a glimpse of what humans look like when we're reflecting God's image in this way. As a species, we long for newness and excitement; we find pleasure in conquering the unknown. We're compelled by what might be. But it is important to frame newness and excitement within God's ongoing work. In *Culture Making*, Andy Crouch writes, "We always start in the middle of things, working with raw materials given to us by God and the generations before us. Culture is what we make of the world, not what we make out of pure imagination."[2] It's grounding, humbling, and at the same time liberating to realize it's not at all about us. Our contribution to this world is part of God's long arc of redemption. In this way, we are connected to all that has come before us and will come after us.

For a while, I led a ministry at my church we affectionately called the *already ministry*. As a ministry team, our job was to look around at what was already happening in our neighborhood and see how we could support it and add value. We passed out candy at the local Halloween block party. We joined a group of volunteers to help clean up the local school. We believed that God was already at work in the happenings of the community.

God is not asking us to redeem the world all by ourselves. God is asking us to amplify the fact that God is redeeming the world. This is not to say that we don't have beautiful ideas and the boldness to carry them through. We are image bearers, after all. It's just that if we're truly bearing God's image, we never start from scratch. We always start in the middle of things.

When I think about how Sarah started Marra Home, I recognize that she started it in the middle of things. She resourced what was already happening in the local communities she came to know—perhaps expecting that God was already at work there. When I asked Sarah about how she had learned to define success, she described nurturing "the identity of people."[3] For Sarah, at the heart of nurturing identity was dignity. Reflecting on the global artisans she hires and sources from, she said,

One way to define success, particularly for what I do and why I do it, is where the people I work with are proud of what they do . . . having a sense of dignity in what they're doing and that they're able to be part of a business that is really powered by the work of their hands and by the history of their people and that is valuable on a world stage and valuable to their families. That it is hopefully something their kids see as still worth doing. That's why these traditional arts stop; it's that they're not making an income and the kids don't see any reason to continue doing them and they're just gone. The society loses that story. It loses quite literally the fabric of their community and what really makes them unique.[4]

I love that Sarah didn't want her work to be a business that taught people new skills. Instead, she wanted to harvest what was already there. That's creativity, and it was difficult for her to trust it at first. But today, as the artisans' traditions are brought to a new market, dignity is redeemed.

Sarah was dialed in to the reality that when we create we always start in the middle of things, we widen our eyes to how God is already at work. This is an especially important point for those of us who will start formal businesses or organizations, as we walk in the entrepreneurial way. Even when we start from scratch, we're really never starting from scratch. Even when we make something out of nothing, we're never quite making something out of nothing. We trust that our creativity is rooted in our capacity to participate with God in making the world new. This means that when inspiration strikes or we create even the most novel of concepts, we trust that it comes from the Spirit dwelling within us.

### *Anticipation*

If creativity is part participation, it is also part *antici-pation*—anticipation of God's final redeemed world.[5] God beckons us to create based on our imagining of a redeemed, restored existence. In this way, it might help to think of our creative work as a foretaste of what might be.[6] It is a common theological expression to say that we live in the tension between the already and the not yet—that God's kingdom is already active and alive in our physical world but that we also expect for the fullness of the kingdom to come into fruition at a time that has not yet come. Our anticipation of God's coming kingdom paves the way for hopeful imagination. We trust that God will indeed renew and redeem the world and turn the seemingly impossible into the possible. In our work, our creativity is part of what might close the gap between what the world is and what the world might be.

Sarah had done a lot of thinking about the relationship between poverty and dignity. Sarah talked about how, yes, money is certainly a core indicator of poverty. But poverty can go much deeper than money and isn't always correlated with it. At the core, poverty threatens our intrinsic value, our identity. She explained that a handcrafted pillow cover might take two weeks for someone to make. Before she started sourcing from these artisan hubs, the makers were forced to sell what they made for whatever they could get.

Tourism being down, sometimes these goods would sell for as little as five bucks. Trading two weeks of work for five dollars was far from ideal. As the goods are continually devalued, the tradition and the community are subject to the same kind of devaluing. But when that same artisan is able to regularly sell their work—in this case on a global stage and at a good price—the craft is not only sentimental but also viable. It's a way for people to make money to feed their families, have a home, and pay for life.

Sarah hoped to be part of the process of God restoring dignity to the communities she met. To me, this is such a great example of what it means to create with anticipation—to create with the belief that a more redeemed, a more just, shalom-filled version of our present circumstances is actually possible. In Sarah's case, hope-filled anticipation looks like her using her God-given resources to partner with artisans to amplify their God-given resources to amplify the intrinsic value of their work. Shalom and justice. These are the fruits of redemption that we can anticipate when we create. Creating with this kind of anticipation beckons us to trust that God is in fact actively redeeming our world.

### Collaboration

Creativity is an act of *collaboration* between human beings. Let's agree to shed the notion that innovations are birthed from the mind of a single genius hunkered down somewhere in a lab or study chamber. Sure, there are rare occasions when individuals come up with brilliant solutions all on their own; however, the vast majority of human creativity is the result of collaborative effort.[7] Even the most seemingly individualistic ideas usually come about as the result of already existing information and structures—often cobbled together over a period of time and sometimes simply formatted in a new way.[8] For example, let's say a man named Robert creates a new app that helps connect people who want to sell furniture with people who want to buy furniture. Robert could argue that he created something without collaborating with others. But in this, he would neglect how the work of so many others paved the way for him. From the technology that makes apps possible to the platform business model that powers so many companies and thus gives a consumer imagination for how his app works—Robert's work is in some ways collaborative with them. That's also not to mention whether he had a graphic designer create a logo for him or whether his spouse works full-time and made it possible for Robert to not make money for a period of time while he developed the app.

We are always jumping into the middle of things—the middle of God's work and those who have come before us.[9] And because God's own trinitarian makeup predicates an understanding of human creativity as collaborative, we can embrace the notion that when we create together we do so with dignity and meaning. When we participate in God's mission, we subject ourselves to God and to one another in a collaborative posture.

One of my most meaningful moments of collaboration came when I worked for a Christian residential counseling center. One of the yearly activities at this center was a two-week backpacking trip in the High Sierras of California. Each day of the trip, two people were picked to lead. Leading meant making decisions about what we would eat, where we would sleep, and generally attending to the other twelve members' needs. It also meant that the trip supervisors pointed to a spot on a topographical map to which the leaders were supposed to navigate by sundown. When it was my day to lead, I was paired with a sixteen-year-old named Ricky.

Because I was the adult and the camp counselor, I assumed that I would be responsible for most of the leading. But when I looked at the map and tried to chart a course for us, I quickly realized I was horrible with the compass. Ricky gently made a few suggestions that revealed he was quite talented with the map and compass. Following his lead, we agreed that he would be in the front charting the course (with occasional check-ins). I would be in the back, watching the group to make sure everyone was okay and on pace. By collaborating with each other, we were both able to bring our full selves to the task and to lean on each other as well. Our individual competencies were challenged, but as we leaned into each other's strengths we created a day that was much better than if either of us had done it alone.

Collaboration is also at the heart of the Marra Home business model. Sarah brings marketing and business skills to the table. The artisans bring the design expertise and product-development operations. Each is dependent on one another to make a profit. Sarah was honest about the complexities of a small yet global operation. She had to learn to add time for the realities of life in Latin America—for instance, during the rainy season when the dye on fabrics can't dry as quickly or when the roads get muddy and trucks can't deliver goods to be shipped.

I love that it reminds me that as a creative worker, I can trust I am not on a solo mission from God. I am part of a larger collective of people who get to join in on God's big mission of redemption, creatively working in anticipation of all that God is doing to make new.

## Creative Confidence

I created a cohort-style experience rooted in my research that is meant to help people wrestle with their most pressing career questions by engaging in the frameworks and activities presented in this book. What has been emphasized in these groups is that, like Molly or myself, many of us have complicated relationships with creativity. We have working definitions in our head of what it means to be creative, and we either opt in or opt out.

Because humans belong to and are made in the image of God, creativity resides within all of us. But the fact that we *are* creative doesn't mean we are always *able* to access or trust our own creative capacity. Sometimes external forces such as systemic inequity make creativity feel like a luxury we don't have. We're exhausted and overwhelmed, and even when we have creative energy it's marginalized in the places we work. Plus, we're too busy surviving; how could we possibly make the space to create? Or maybe it's not that we feel marginalized but we just feel too vulnerable to expose our most creative ideas—and therefore ourselves—to the harsh critique of the world. We fear being thought of as unprofessional or not serious enough. Or maybe we're very in touch with our creativity, but our experience is that going there demands so much from us. We struggle with trusting what feels like a wild beast that doesn't have room to run.

Think about it: *Does creativity come naturally to you? Or do you have to work at it? Does the environment you work in celebrate or squash creativity? How have your work contexts impacted your creative confidence?*

In the cohorts, I have seen many people wrestle out loud with these questions, which often leads to generative and transformative inner work. As people wrestle, I've noticed two fears that seem to hold people back from trusting their creativity. These of course aren't the only fears that hold us back, but I've heard them enough that they're worth playing out here. They are *the fear of not living the life we imagine others are living* and *the fear of being judged*. I've observed these fears hold others and myself back time and time again.

### Face the Fear of Not Living the Life We Imagine Others Are Living

One of the most prevalent fears that can inhibit creativity is popularly known as FOMO—the fear of missing out. Let me illustrate with a story from my own life.

On more than one occasion, I've had a younger woman approach me after a lecture or speaking engagement and ask with doe-like eyes, "How do you do it all?" Over time, I've learned that this question is short for "How do you work and mother and write and speak? How do you balance work and life?" Whenever I am asked this question, I gently grab the shoulders of the woman in front of me, look her square in the eyes, and let her in on my secret: *I don't do it all*. I've learned the hard way that I cannot spin all the plates. I've only got two hands.

Right in that moment, I admit to the woman in front of me that my choice to be with her and the others in the room might mean that the dishes are piling up at home or that I'm going to be thirty minutes later to preschool pickup than I would like or that my hair is doused in dry shampoo.

This is not to say that the pendulum also doesn't swing the other way. If I take the day off from my paid work and focus exclusively on the work of motherhood, I'll likely amass an unruly stack of emails in my inbox. Because I do it too, I know that these young women will shape their vision of the life they want based on how they see other women living. The problem with this is that we only see small slices of one another's lives. We then use those glimpses to construct our hoped-for realities based on those small parts, not on the entire picture.

When we construct our visions of a good life based on the small parts we see of other people's lives, we chance constructing what we hope for on something that might not even be possible. We simply don't have all the pieces. And perhaps unknowingly, we might fill in the gaps between things we see in other people's lives with ideas that aren't real or possible. We might imagine that a woman who seems like she is rocking her job is doing it stress-free when in reality she feels overwhelmed. Or we might imagine that a successful man has had a smooth route to get there, when in fact he's had to overcome many obstacles. The truth is, we have no idea. When we develop a vision for our lives on what we imagine to be true about others, we're building our expectations on limited information.

Over and over again, I've seen that building our expectations for our future based on small parts of other people's lives can breed fear. I've seen it in myself. This is not to say that we shouldn't model our behavior after those who've come before us. But we do need to approach that modeling with a kind of grace for ourselves that helps us lean into creative confidence instead of fear.

### *Face the Fear of Being Judged*

This next story highlights that I am a hypocrite. For all the strong words I have for young women about not attempting to do it all, I have a hard time following my own advice. One of the things I've sensed God has called me to do is write. Lately, this calling has gotten audible in my head—not so loud that I hear an audible voice I think is God's. Instead, it sounds like the ringing of an analog telephone, as if someone were literally calling me on the phone. The longer I rush around tending to everything else but the phone, the louder the ringing gets.

As I've sensed God inviting me deeper into the work of writing, I've dug into the work of other writers I admire. I've read everything they've ever written. And based on my perception of those small parts of their lives, I construct hopes for my own vocational journey. Yes, I fear not living the life I imagine they are living, but it goes further. I fear being judged. I fear that I will create and try to hope and imagine, but people won't like it, won't like me. My brain starts to spiral with fears: *What if I skip a trip to the park with my kids only to write a bunch of words that are shallow and meaningless? What if I think my ideas are great, but everyone else is confused or disinterested? What if this big idea I have in my head doesn't actually work out?*

And when all of these fears get loud, they seem to drown out the telephone in my head. When this happens, I do nothing. I certainly do not create. I spiral downward and inward into insecurity instead of putting one foot in front of the other toward faithfulness. So yes, sometimes I lose my nerve, I cry in the shower, and I give up. This fear inhibits my creative confidence.

I've heard many people describe how out of control the world feels. Whether it's in politics and lawmaking, in our families and our work, we face taxing amounts of unpredictability and chaos. It's exponentially disorienting and difficult when the systems we live and work in are biased against us. So it's natural that in the midst of all this overwhelm, we would sometimes crave control—not because we are power hoarding or evil people but because the chaos of the world is hard, especially when we're trying to make sense of God's callings. We just want to be able to breathe. Relax. Create margin.

We're certainly not in control of God's callings. We're probably not even in control of how our work trajectory has unfolded up until the present. And if we're being honest, we probably realize that we're not in control of how things will unfold from here on out.

In the face of chaos, it might feel counterintuitive to lean into our creative core. This is because when we lean into creativity we also have to let go. But that's exactly what the entrepreneurs in my research knew how to do. In the face of great needs—even in the face of true chaos—they had to relinquish control in order to subject themselves to the creative process of experimentation and iteration that enabled them to address the needs they sensed God calling them to work on.

## Rest and Trust That God Is Near

The same biblical narrative that tells us about the creation of the world and of human beings also tells us about the relationship between creative work and rest. Genesis 2 opens with a picture of Creator God being finished with breathing life into the world. Then verse 3 says this: "Then God blessed the seventh day and made it holy, because on it he rested from all the work of creating that he had done." This day of rest after work is commonly called the *Sabbath*. As humans, we're supposed to mirror not only God's act of creativity but also the rest that is modeled for us in Genesis. Rest is a gift of creation. Our participation in rest is a sign of our trust that God is in charge and we as humans are not. There is a natural rhythm of work and rest built into many aspects of how God designed the world and us. I suppose I first really learned this lesson by watching corn grow.

I grew up in a city of about a half-million people, a midsize city mostly made up of houses and shops and other suburban amenities. But just outside the city in nearly any direction you'd find agriculture of various kinds. A large swath of the year was measured by the production of corn. In summer, the mantra was that corn would be "knee high by the fourth of July." In August, farmers loaded up their freshly harvested corn and drove into the city to sell it out of the backs of pickup trucks. And by late September, the leftover stalks in the field turned golden brown. Although I've never picked an ear of corn in my life, the rhythm of planting, growing, harvesting, and dormancy is forever sketched into the aesthetics of my brain. And that aesthetic has shaped my own expectation for my work. I trust the rhythm of what I have seen, that there is a time for planting, a time for growing, a time for harvesting, and a time to clear the fields and let the ground rest. And of course, it's not just corn. Summer turns to fall that turns to winter and then eventually spring and summer. Day turns to night and then back to day again.

Our bodies demand sleep every single day. Our brains crave rest on the heels of a day's hard work.

In the relentlessness of our always-on, on-demand culture, we've lost a healthy rhythm between work and rest. Our computers can always be on. Our phones are always charged. There is always more to do. And rest goes by the wayside. Author Wayne Muller writes,

> Our culture invariably supposes that action and accomplishment are better than rest, that doing something—anything—is better than doing nothing. Because of our desire to succeed, to meet these ever-growing expectations, we do not rest. Because we do not rest, we lose our way.[10]

Frenetically fixated on doing things, we often miss what's most important. Because we don't rest, we don't recalibrate. And when we don't recalibrate, we lose our way. Why on earth would we do this? A friend and I were talking recently about how easy it is not to rest. He was telling me how the fact that he could listen to a podcast while driving while also thinking about an upcoming meeting made him feel exhausted because he was everywhere at once and therefore nowhere really at all. The truth is this is part of the changing nature of work. The same systems that make it easy to communicate and share information make it hard to turn work off. And it's not just that we're bad or undisciplined people. Our systems glorify productivity and profit to the point that we think it honorable to make personal sacrifices in the name of work.

Living like this undermines so much. It threatens to warp our self-images as people too closely associated with our doing (when we know God is also interested in our being). It threatens to undermine our health. We're not made to work all the time. It's not our natural rhythm as species. And ironically, not resting actually undermines our creativity. When we're pushed to work beyond measure, we end up either over-trusting our capacities or undervaluing our creativity because we never stop to fuel up.

A colleague who is a professor told me that one of the most valuable lessons she learned on a semester-long sabbatical was that she was in fact replicable. At first, I thought I must have misheard her. Replaceable? How could that be a good thing? She explained that when she realized the weight of the world was not on her shoulders, she was able to lean into healthier rhythms of work and rest. The by-product? She was more creative and more productive.

We're at the point as a society when rest is an act of resistance. This is well documented by everyone—from theologians like Walter Bruggemann to popular Instagram accounts like the Nap Ministry. Rooted in the resistance is an assertion of trust in God over ourselves. Because we trust that God is near, we can stop. Because we trust the rhythm of how God created the world (and us), we can model our own rhythms in suit.

I have learned that God's invitation to rest is part a tool of subversion and part an act of loving care. When we stop and put down our hammer or our pen, our stethoscope or our work gloves, we are acknowledging that we trust God, not ourselves. For me, God's most important calls to rest come right when I can't possibly imagine taking a break. This invitation comes in sometimes surprising ways. On the eve of a big deadline, when I feel so tired I could cry, the soft whisper of my child's voice beckons me to dance or read or play make-believe. When the house is full of dishes and dust after a long day of work, my hiking boots seem to jump out from their place in my closet, inviting me to walk instead of work. Sometimes I recognize these moments as the invitation they are, and sometimes I ignore them flat out. I am almost never rewarded when I just push through. On the contrary, when I'm able to step away and rest and even play, God restores my energy both by reminding me that God is God and I am not and by giving me fresh eyes when I return to my work.

Rest is part of the rhythm of creation. Our willingness to rest is a sign of our trust in God. As part of our invitation to trust that we are creative, we're invited to rest and know that God is near—to delight in the work God is doing that extends far beyond our own hands. Resting invites us to mirror God's own creation rhythm. Our belonging to God and mirroring God's image allows us to draw creative confidence that helps us participate creatively with what God is up to in the world.

## EXERCISE: Trust Fall

So much of creativity requires trust. Trusting God enough to rest. Trusting that God has indeed made us creative—even if we don't always believe it. Trusting that God has made other people creative, inviting us to approach people with curiosity and to lean into collaboration.

Growing up, I played softball. We went on yearly team-building retreats. There was always a trust fall. Maybe you've done this exercise. It's when a team of people interweave their arms and create a human net for someone else to blindly fall backward on.

This exercise is like a trust fall—but don't worry, you don't have to blindly fall backward into a group of middle school girls' arms. Instead, you're going to think about what makes you feel confident and what makes you feel scared when it comes to your own creativity. Put another way, you're going to check in with yourself to see how you currently trust your creativity and where there might be room for growth.

Take several minutes to journal on the following questions. Focus on those that feel most helpful for you.

1. Describe a time when you felt creative.
2. Describe a time when you doubted your creativity.
3. In what areas of your life do you feel comfortable bringing your creativity?
4. In what areas of your life do you feel like you have to hold back?
5. Does rest come easily to you? Or do you have to work at it?

# Build Resilience

I've had my fair share of setbacks in work. If I'm honest, there have been more than a handful of moments that still make me want to heave. Take for example what happened while I was working on my PhD. In order to get a PhD, I had to write a dissertation. My dissertation was supposed to prove that I could make a "unique and valuable" contribution to my field of practical theology. A set of advisors, referred to as *my committee*, coached me through the process and ultimately judged my work.

I started doing the heavy lifting of writing my dissertation when my daughter was just eight months old. Contrary to the instincts of any new parent, I'd set my alarm to wake up when it was still dark just to get a few hours of writing in before she woke up. Then I'd write during her naps and again late into the night. I was basically a hot mess, but I loved what I was writing. I thought it was original and inspired and helpful.

Halfway through my project, I had a review meeting with my committee. That morning, I put on my favorite gold blazer, black dress pants, and heels. My husband did my daughter's entire morning routine so that I could take my time getting ready. As I headed out the door, he told me that he had bought a nice bottle of wine and the ingredients to make a good dinner. We had both earned a night of celebration—a pause from the breakneck pace that my writing had put us on.

At the meeting, I had my laptop out, ready to receive my committee's notes. I expected some minor criticism, but mostly I expected them to join me in excitement about my work. I was proud of what I had done.

However, as the conversation moved beyond the opening chitchat, a sinking feeling grew in my stomach. I realized what kind of meeting this was going to be—the kind I had heard about but had never imagined would happen to me. This was the meeting where your committee told you that your work wasn't strong enough. This was the meeting where your committee told you that you had to start over. They were empathetic and kind. But their good manners did little to blunt the blow of the truth. I was going to have to throw 125 pages in the trash! There's no way I would make up the time. Graduation would be put off another year. My career goals would be put off another year. Our family goals of having a second child—those would have to wait as well.

To this day, I have no idea how I made it through the rest of that meeting without completely breaking down. As I shut the door on my way out, grief came crashing in like a wave.

I could no longer hold back my tears—they came streaming down my cheeks uncontrollably and forcefully. I ran down two flights of steps, out the front door, and to my car. I sat in the driver's seat clutching my laptop and sobbing hard, honest, angry tears.

I thought my work was strong. It was not. I thought they were going to love it. They did not. I hadn't just misread the moment; I had misjudged my entire project. I had failed—quite significantly. I was embarrassed, discouraged, and disoriented. It was a setback that I certainly didn't expect, and it was one I didn't know if I could recover from. At the very least, all of my goals would have to wait just a bit longer.

What I now know but couldn't have seen then is that God was inviting me into a process of holy wrestling and honest inner work that would set the stage for the next several years of my life and work. At the heart of it, God was inviting me to grow in resilience. In fact, experts argue that resilience is the most important skill workers need in a changing world.[1] Formally defined, *resilience* is the ability not only to endure setbacks and stress but also to learn and perform well in light of them.[2]

The idea that resilience is the most important skill we need for work is rather sobering—both because it signals how much more disruption, unpredictability, and setback are on the horizon and because the hard truth about resilience is that it's hard earned. We earn a badge of resilience by enduring and learning to thrive in the midst of tough circumstances. In this, getting honest is critical—we expect work and all of life to be a dance of highs and lows. We anticipate that our work will at least at times be heartbreakingly tough. And so we fix our eyes on developing the entrepreneurial muscle of resilience, which I believe has a lot to do with the Christian concept of resurrection.

## Resilience and Resurrection

In the last chapter, I made the case that because God is by nature creative and because we are made in the image of God, we are made to be creative. It is in our bones. If our capacity to create is rooted in our first story about God, then our capacity to be resilient is found in our climactic story in Christ. Resilience is a gift of resurrection.

Jesus was put to death on a cross on a Friday. He was exposed and ridiculed and condemned. A handful of followers laid him to rest in a tomb. But when a couple of faithful women went to the tomb to tend to his body on Sunday, he was no longer there. God had raised him from the dead. God had exalted him, and he was with God, having received the promise of the Holy Spirit to pour out. Death does not have the final word in God's kingdom. What this means for us is that when we're in the midst of suffering setback, wondering and waiting, we can trust that God is present—that God is breaking into our pain. The assurance that death does not have the final word helps us hope for what might be and believe that new life is possible. When we orient our everyday actions around the hope of resurrection, we build up the muscles of resilience.

So much of life—including our work—mirrors the resurrection arc. When we experience setback, change, and loss, we're living in the wake of Good Friday. When we're grieving what was and hoping for what might be, we're in the holding pattern of Holy Saturday. And when we experience new life sprouting on the heels of pain, we're invited by God to delight in the surprise and joy of Easter Sunday. I like to think of the everyday moments when our work and our lives mirror the resurrection arc as *small r resurrection* moments.

I eventually did get to work on rewriting my dissertation after that painful meeting. Though I didn't really know where to start or what to do, I did hope that God would redeem what felt like such an epic failure. But I also knew that I had to show up, and I knew I had to listen to others. I had to get in there and try—even if I failed again.

One night after a long day of rewriting, I settled in to watch some TV with my then two-year-old daughter. As I held her on my lap, I noticed a small red dot on her earlobe. It wasn't exactly a scratch; it was more like someone had taken a red pen and dotted her lobe. It was weird enough that I showed my husband, and we agreed to keep an eye on it.

Within a week, the dot had grown in size, and we decided to take her to the doctor. Our doctor didn't know what the spot was, so she referred us to a specialist. While we waited for the appointment with the specialist, the spot morphed into a lump. The specialist said she had never seen anything quite like it before. She took some pictures and put calls in to her doctor friends. If I'm honest, it felt pretty alarming to have so many smart doctors have no idea what was wrong with my kid.

A few days after the appointment with the specialist, the lump had doubled in size and I was done playing it cool. It was the Wednesday before Easter, and we went back in to see the specialist. She took one look at how much the lump had grown and immediately sent us to see a team at Los Angeles Children's Hospital.

It was holy week—the day before Maundy Thursday, two days before Good Friday—and two weeks before I was set to defend my newly revised dissertation.

The new doctors told us that our daughter had a tumor, very possibly cancer. They would need to biopsy it. They encouraged us to go and enjoy Easter and come back to see them the following week. The biopsy would happen on a Thursday. I was scheduled to defend my dissertation the following Monday, and we'd get the results about the tumor that same week on Thursday. It felt surreal that my dissertation defense was sandwiched directly between the biopsy and the diagnosis. It would have made good sense to postpone my defense, but one of my committee members couldn't meet for another eight weeks if we did. At that point, I just needed that project done. Right then and there, I gave myself permission to cry through the entire defense if I needed to. I was done holding back my tears.

The anguish of Good Friday, the waiting of Holy Saturday, and the hope of Easter Sunday took on new meaning for me that year. I thought about Mother Mary as she watched her baby boy die on a cross. I thought about how she must have wailed and wondered and waited to see him again. I thought about how overwhelmed or numb or angry she must have felt. Probably heartbroken but maybe also weirdly proud— that the work he came to do was finished. Was she expecting the Resurrection? Could she even imagine it?

A few months earlier, I had wondered how I was going to come back from that midpoint meeting. Since then, I had poured so much into rewriting and had worked so hard to make up for lost time. I was convinced that I could muscle myself across the finish line. I had convinced myself that a successful defense would be my resurrection moment—the moment that earned me a badge of resilience. But try as I might, I could not muscle my way to resurrection. I could not roll away the stone from my own tomb or ensure my own future would be bright. God is always the source of resurrection.

If we trust that God is the source of resurrection, then we can believe that even when our world turns upside down, we gain nothing by white knuckling for control. And because of the hope that a setback never has the final word, leaning in and letting go are actually possible. Remember, letting go isn't a mark of passivity but rather of deep acceptance that, try as we might, we cannot control the upside-down elements of life.

A day before my daughter's biopsy, I was driving in the same car I had wept in a few months earlier. Looking back, it's almost as if that car was my proverbial tomb—the place that held the death of my expectations and grief about all that was happening. As I exited off the interstate and turned onto a road I drive nearly every day, I felt God sprout new life in me. I can count on one hand the times in my life that I've heard audible words from God. That's just not how God mostly speaks to me. We've got other ways of communicating. But right there, when my daughter's well-being was on the line and all I had worked for professionally felt clouded in chaos, God invited me again to lean in and let go. In that darkness and waiting held by that tomb of a car, without any assurance of how things would turn out, I felt the hope of love and comfort and peace.

For me, the badge of resilience wasn't reserved for when I eventually passed my defense. It didn't even come when we got the news that our daughter was going to be fine—that the tumor in her ear was in fact not a tumor but a calcified hair follicle. Basically, she had an angry zit. No, resilience was a gift that came by way of the small *r* resurrection moment. It was just as surprising as it was peaceful. It came in the form of perspective, bursting in through that tomb of a car as I drove on a familiar street going to a familiar place.

If you lose your job, your badge of resilience isn't suspended until you get a new one. If you fail a big project, resurrection doesn't have to take the shape of a successful achievement later on. If you have a fallout with a colleague, resurrection may come long before reconciliation. If you feel heartbroken and overwhelmed and like you're in a tomb—know that Sunday is indeed coming. God moves toward you in your pain because you are loved. You will not be left in the tomb of grief forever. Light, perspective, and new life will inevitably break through.

### Embrace Setback

Knowing that scholars see resiliency as so key to a new world of work and feeling it so deeply in my own life, I wondered what entrepreneurs could teach us about dealing with setbacks. It's why I asked people about success *and* failure in my research. There's a lot in the literature about how entrepreneurs and innovators tend to prioritize failing early, learning, and iterating, all in search of innovative and meaningful work. But I wanted to hear about it for myself.

When I asked entrepreneurs about success and failure, the common theme was that they were *much* more comfortable talking about failures than they were successes. When trying to define success, nearly all the folks I interviewed were noticeably uncomfortable or hesitant. Some even had a hard time articulating their thoughts. Most were unsure how much success they had actually achieved and instead wanted to talk about all they still imagined for the future. They'd point to some things that had worked, but that wasn't what they wanted to linger on. After a few of these conversations, I realized that these people, whom I perceived as interesting and successful, weren't just being weirdly modest.

When I asked these same people to talk about failures, they loosened up. They talked openly and freely, easily recounting examples of pain they accidently caused, choices that led to a loss in money, or risks that completely back-fired. They were honest about how painful these failures had been—both for them and for others. But in spite of the pain, they were so comfortable with the idea of learning and iteration that they didn't even want to use the word *failure*. One man suggested that this word elicited too much negativity and finality. He preferred to think about the things that didn't go as planned more as learning opportunities.

People's comfort with success and failure has become a litmus test for me. When I ask people I meet how they've learned to define success and failure and what practices have moved them toward success and helped them deal with failure, I know that I want to spend more time with people who embrace setback rather than those who run from it. My favorite kinds of people are those who talk about failure and setback honestly and vulnerably but without degrading to a place of shame or blame.

Take for example Amy Kaherl, the founder of Detroit Soup, a nonprofit that helps facilitate crowdfunded micro grants to creative projects across the Detroit area. The organization has facilitated nearly $150,000 of community investment across various neighborhoods in Detroit, which is especially notable as the average donor contributes $5.[3] The model has spread to over 170 locations around the world.[4] Amy has been written about in the *New York Times*, and the BBC did a documentary on Detroit Soup. Amy was even honored by the Obama administration.[5] Talk about life goals.

When I asked Amy about how she had learned to define success, she candidly told me that many other people consider her and Detroit Soup successful. But she wrestled with the idea of how to truly measure success. She was proud of the mission and how well they'd advanced it, but she was honest in saying that due to the nature of the organization, it wasn't exactly making her rich—nor was that the point. She'd struggled with how to make it more financially viable for her as a leader. Fundraising had been hard, and she didn't want to raise the at-the-door price because the $5 cost of admission was already enough of a risk for many of the folks who came out. She said it was nice that other people thought it was successful but lamented that it couldn't be all that she envisioned.[6]

Then I asked Amy to define failure. Whereas she struggled a bit with how to frame and evaluate success, she was much more sure about and comfortable with failure. Amy said, "Success, I don't know, but failure feels like when I can't move the project to the next level or move it to the place where I have the vision for it to go."[7] In Amy, I heard a familiarity with failure that enabled a healthy embrace of setback and also enabled her to wrestle with common images of success. It's part of why I immediately liked her so much, and it's what made me think I had a lot to learn from her. I can imagine that not achieving what she envisioned was discouraging, disorienting, and even painful. But her comfort in talking about setback led me to believe that she had a fruitful relationship with it. That she in her own words and own ways had learned to spot the small *r* resurrection moments in the work of Detroit Soup. Embracing setback requires a willingness to get intimate with loss. Intimacy with loss creates an ecosystem in which God can cultivate new life in ways that build our muscles of resilience.

Joanna Waterfall is the founder of Yellow Collective, a business that works toward "empowering creative, entrepreneurial women to become agents of good."[8] When I asked Joanna about how she's learned to define failure, she told me a story.

Several years ago, Yellow embarked on a campaign to raise $60,000 for a new website. They did so through the crowdfunding platform Kickstarter. For months, her team put countless hours into strategy, marketing, and fundraising for the campaign. But ultimately, they came up short; they didn't meet their $60,000 goal. And because Kickstarter is an all-or-nothing platform, they returned their investors' money. If you've ever been involved in or even watched someone run a crowdfunding campaign from afar, you know it is basically a full-time job. When Yellow fell short of their goal, Joanna was heartbroken. All that work for nothing. She would have to find another way or postpone that dream. Joanna told me that when they didn't hit their goal, she was honestly shocked. She really hadn't imagined they would come up short. They had such a vibrant, faithful community of supporters, so this felt surprising.

Joanna described what came next as critical. She and her team decided to host a fail party—a time for their vibrant, faithful community of supporters to come out and celebrate that they had taken a risk, that they had tried, that they had vulnerably put themselves into the world. Sure, it felt tough to fail, but for Joanna, failure was a symbol of bravery, not of defeat.

Joanna went on to tell me that after the Kickstarter fail, she became a lot less afraid to take risks. This was a small r resurrection moment. This is resiliency in action. This is the fruit of new life having sprouted. She explained that the process of trying and hoping and coming up short had cemented the fact that while she loves the things she does, she is not defined by them. Her value as a human *being* is not dependent on her human *doing*. Now when she approaches things, she's much more prone to think, "All right. Let's try this. We'll put it out there, and if it fails I'm still me. You're still you. We'll learn more, and it will be okay."[9]

Even when we fail, we'll be okay. You'll still be you, and I'll still be me. Chances are that if we can embrace setback and trust that it holds opportunity for growth, we can step into more of whoever it is God is calling us to become. And chances are that we won't always fail. Sometimes those risks—whether they're giant or tiny—will prove to be the next step on our journey to wherever God is calling us to go.

## Grief Will Set You Free

The path to liberation in a changing world of work comes through wholehearted grief. Grief helps us name what we've lost. It helps us get honest about what we long for. Grief gives way to creativity. It is also a means of harnessing the big feelings of death to make way for new life.

As I talk with entrepreneurs, they tell stories of loss and failure that really do feel like a type of death. It might sound dramatic to equate the stuff of our work lives with death. And this certainly isn't meant to trivialize the actual death of people we know or love. It's just to say that when what we do matters to us and something ends or fails or gets taken away, it is natural to experience these moments like a type of death.

Take for example Stephen, who owns a tech company. Stephen described to me that he had always wanted his company to go public. In order to achieve this goal, he knew early on he'd have a list of milestones he would need to hit along the way. But year after year, Stephen failed to hit these milestones. He'd get close sometimes, but no matter how hard he tried or how clever his tactics were, the goals felt elusive. When we talked, he no longer imagined that his company could go public. Stephen explained that he had to face the death of that hope and grieve unfulfilled dreams or he was at risk of too much fear settling in. He didn't want a fear of failure to guide his decisions. He didn't want to live and work as a man who doubted himself. That didn't fit with his model of faithfulness to God in his work. As we talked, I was convinced that God had worked in a small *r* resurrection way and that Stephen had been receptive to God's work.

My ability to embrace setback and thus strengthen my own resilience muscles has hinged on my ability to face my *fear* of failure. My ability to face my fear of failure has hinged on my capacity to grieve. In some areas of my life, I'd say that I'm fairly risk tolerant—that I'm okay if I don't get things right. But there are other areas of my life where I cringe at the idea of failing. It's especially hard for me when I perceive myself as coming up short as a mother or when I think I let my people down as a leader.

During a particularly challenging season of leadership, my mom wisely asked me, "Why are you afraid to fail?" I waded through a bunch of half sentences until I admitted, "I don't want to fail because I'm afraid of who that means I am. Basically, my identity is at stake." Even though I know in my bones that my *being* is more of an identity marker than my *doing*, what I do is still really important to me. And I believe that because God calls us to work, God cares about my doing. While in my head I know that failure is not only permissible but also important for creativity, it doesn't take the sting out of failure. My mom pointed out that it sounded as though I wasn't trying to avoid the failure itself but rather the pain and shame that come with it. That felt so true.

Maybe you're like me and your capacity to tolerate failure is linked with how personally invested you are in a relationship or a project. In other words, if we are only a little bit invested in something, the pain of failure doesn't sting as much. In fact, we might be fine to fail and iterate all day long for things we're only loosely involved in. But the more we care about an idea, a relationship, or a dream, the more painful it is when things do not work out.

This fear is what threatens the deep and meaningful kind of work we crave. If we always keep one foot out to protect ourselves from pain, we never experience the joy of a life lived all the way in.

Like Stephen, in order to deal with failure, we have to learn to deal with death. At first glance, death is uncomfortable, hard, painful, and scary. We find it difficult to sit still with the pain that seeps in when things don't turn out the way we imagined or when we feel as if we've let people down. But understanding failure as a type of death helps us to hold on to the promise that the tomb is not permanent. It helps us to sit in the uncomfortable space that our human soul craves in the midst of chaos—the grief that loss requires. God knows death. God conquers death. God helps us know that death is part of life—that on the heels of it come the small seeds of new resurrection life.

### Grieving When Our Experience Doesn't Match Our Expectations

The first time David and I met was at an outdoor café near my house. As we sipped our coffee, I asked him a bit about his story. He started by telling me about his parents—how they had been his biggest cheerleaders growing up. He talked about how they had helped him believe that someday he could be anything he wanted to be.

Encouraged to pick a career path that lined up with his passions, he got a degree in journalism. David had always loved to write, so this seemed like a natural choice. After school, he tried to get a full-time job at a newspaper. He learned quickly that the news industry was changing fast, including how journalists were hired and paid. Unable to land the full-time job he imagined, he wound up freelancing. He worked tons of hours and was paid by the article. The more he got published, the more money he made. But none of the gigs paid very well, so David found himself writing up to twenty articles a week—some of which never got published and he never got paid for. The money just wasn't worth all the work he was doing. Plus, he had $80,000 in student loans and $10,000 in credit card debt, not to mention his regular monthly bills. He decided that the freelance life just wasn't worth the stress it caused. Instead, David took a job as a copyeditor for a marketing firm. When we met for coffee, he had been doing that job for nearly three years. In that time, he'd been promoted and was now a senior copyeditor.

When I asked David how he liked being a senior copyeditor, he took a slow sip of coffee before he answered. As he set his cup down on the outdoor picnic table we sat at, he confessed, "I hate my job. Well, I don't totally hate it . . . I guess I just don't like it. It just doesn't feel like me." Sighing, he added, "Actually, it's sort of the worst. But I know not everyone has a job that pays the bills, so I should stop complaining. If I'm honest, I hate my job, but I'm embarrassed to feel this way. I feel like such a whiny white guy."

David went on to tell me that he craved work that mattered but felt trapped by his degree and career choices. He loved to write but didn't love writing so that businesses could sell more products people didn't need. David was sure he wanted to do something else but had a hard time imagining what that would even be. Plus, he described how the world was changing and that the idea of justice and equity were important to him in ways that weren't on his radar when he was younger. He wanted to figure out how to weave that conviction in with his work.

David was caught in the tension between expectations and lived reality that I've heard many people talk about in different ways. Most of us develop certain visions for our lives—whether we can articulate them or not. So it's kind of crushing when life and work don't play out like we expected. We wonder, *Am I not good enough? What went wrong? What am I missing? How do I get back on track? Where do I really belong? Who am I deep down? What's my actual purpose?* Much of this comes down to the fact that our collective expectations are calibrated for a world filled with career escalators and step-by-step instructions on how to get ahead in life. But here we are in our little kayaks, making our way in a white-water-rapid world—a world marked by constant and unpredictable change.

Sometimes we have to grieve what never was. We have to grieve for the path or the profession that felt like a good bet but didn't turn out to be fruitful in the way we imagined. Sometimes we have to grieve the fact that the meaning we sought was overshadowed by dysfunctional systems or systemic bias. That's hard. In this, we see that part of the work of building resilience is preparing to be unprepared and expecting the unexpected.

Rebecca's story is a bit different. For years, she and I have had conversations about how we would approach the role of motherhood alongside our work. At first, our conversations were filled with hypothetical imaginings of what it might be like for us each to become a mom who also has a job we love in our respective industries. *Could we do both? Would we want to do both? How exactly would that work?* But as the months and eventually years went by, our conversations turned from wondering how we would do it all to wondering why Rebecca wasn't getting pregnant. Our conversations took an even different tone as Rebecca and her husband, Brian, dealt with years of painful and unexplained infertility.

Eventually, with the help of some incredible doctors, Rebecca did get pregnant and have a baby. I can still remember my sense of relief when she hit certain milestones in that pregnancy. I imagined that all would finally be well when their baby boy made his way into the world. As his due date approached, Rebecca planned to take maternity leave and maybe even some extended time off from work. She and Brian decided that his work as an adjunct professor would be enough to get them by for a while. Rebecca gave birth to her son in 2020, which means she gave birth against the backdrop of a global pandemic. As if not having Brian in the delivery room and having to wear a mask for thirty hours of labor wasn't enough, Brian's work evaporated overnight. Because Brian was on the seniority list, when schools started to cut costs he was the first to go. Their vision for life as new parents was anything but on track.

In those first few months, baby Charlie didn't sleep well, cried a lot, and demanded more from Rebecca than she ever knew was possible. The transition to parenthood can be so rough. Amid their transition, Rebecca had to go back to work right after maternity leave. They could no longer afford for her to take the extended time off they had wanted. Brian stayed home with the baby, which he was glad to do, but he couldn't help feeling bad that he couldn't muster up more work.

Rebecca's and my conversations about work and motherhood evolved once again. She confided in me that even though she imagined loving her time with baby Charlie, she didn't really like the repetitive work of taking care of a new baby. But she felt guilty about not liking it because of how much she had longed for a child and because she and Brian had planned for her to stay home for a while. Truthfully, part of her was glad to be working. But at the same time, she longed for more time with her baby. Both she and Brian were overwhelmed and increasingly discouraged.

Rebecca was balancing more than is reasonable. Amid the dreams and losses and starts and stops, she and Brian wrestled with how they could balance it all—how they could provide for their family and both be working in the ways they imagined themselves doing. They were grieving that their experience didn't match their expectations. And they were grieving that the ground had shifted beneath them.

### Grieving When the Ground Shifts beneath Us

Sometimes change comes fast. Sometimes we feel as though the ground is shifting beneath us, kind of like when Brian's work evaporated overnight because of a global pandemic. Embracing this kind of change can feel like trying to give a hug to someone during a massive earthquake.

I felt the ground shift beneath me on a cold February morning in Los Angeles. My son was six weeks old. We were in that fragile phase of life marked by milk-stained shirts, endless baby bouncing, and room-temperature coffee. That day, a good friend sent me a text. She was both a good friend and a client of ours through Long Winter. We were partway into a large project, rebranding the company she owned. I hadn't checked in on the project in weeks because of, well, milk stains and room-temp coffee. I was supposed to be on leave, but she wanted to come over. I agreed so long as she was cool with entering our newborn chaos.

As she sat at the edge of our woven grey couch, I noticed how worn the cushions looked underneath her body. My mind drifted to cushion stuffing as I bounced my son in my arms. I rolled up the sleeves of my oversized sweatshirt and turned my attention back to her. I pulled back my son's blanket to show her that he was wearing one of the outfits she had given us—a hand-me-down first worn by her son.

As she started talking, the light poured in through a nearby window, highlighting the heaviness in her eyes. She was quick to the point: she was canceling her project with us halfway through. In her words, our work had missed the mark—and if she was honest, she should have severed the relationship much earlier. Our style turned out not to be what she was looking for. As I shifted my son from one arm to the other, she looked straight at me and told me that I had poorly managed the working relationship. She said that the project had suffered from my underinvolvement.

My face turned hot with anger. Partly I was mad because I didn't see things as she did. But I was also mad because she had come into our sacred and tender space to deliver the news. I got fired in my living room while holding my newborn son. Yes, you could say that I've had better days.

I can own that I was underinvolved. I can own that I didn't set clear expectations. I can own that my work didn't deliver what she needed. Plus, she's a good person—a really good person. I'm sure that moment was really hard for her. I've had to let people go too. That's how I know I wasn't the only one who'd had better days.

Recovering from that moment required much grief work. We had counted on that income. We thought our work was good. I love my friend. The ground shifted beneath us in a way that would never quite go back to being the same. A year and a half later, though we've talked, life has made it so that I still haven't seen my friend face-to-face. I trust that time will come, and I look forward to it. But again, resurrection isn't reserved for when I see her and hug her and ask her about her kids. God has been healing and sprouting new life all along.

How do we look for the small *r* resurrection moments when the ground shifts beneath us? How do we ensure that instead of pain causing us to become hardened, it helps us cultivate resiliency? Father Richard Rohr, a celebrated spiritual teacher and Franciscan priest, says that if we do not transform our pain, we will transmit it.[10] I'm increasingly convinced that this kind of transformation comes in partnership with God—a partnership in which we are willing to do hard work. We must be willing to do the holy wrestling that inevitably gives way to resiliency, which helps us boldly continue our creative pursuit of joining in God's redeeming work in the world.

It also helps to know that God is present in our troubles. Psalm 46 tells us that because God is a "very present help in trouble," we don't have to fear "though the earth should change, though the mountains shake in the heart of the sea" (vv. 1–2). These verses helps us to see that while we can never quite prepare for an earthquake, we should expect that earthquakes are indeed coming. The ground will shift beneath us. We will have days when everything feels like it changed. But God is a *very present help*. God is helpful in providing both refuge from the quaking earth and strength to face whatever changes are taking place. And in this, we have the invitation not to fear.

There are times when the ground shifts beneath us. There are times when our experiences don't match our expectations. There are times when we fail and when what we hoped for dies. We build our resilience muscles by doing two things at the same time: honestly embracing the pain of life and fully hoping for what might be. Grief is a gift that reminds us that we are fully alive, that we're full of big feelings, human tenderness, and love. Hope is a choice—a choice we're compelled to make as people who live in the wake of the Resurrection and all its resurrection implications.

## EXERCISE: Write a Lament

It's not always easy to step into grief. It's not always easy to know what to do or what to say. This is why I love the psalms of lament. This collection of songs scattered through the book of Psalms shows us that to grieve is biblical, that anger can be righteous, and that God meets us in our grief. By cultivating a regular practice of lamenting, we strengthen our capacity to grieve and hope. We live into our creed as a Friday-Saturday-Sunday people.

Though I had known about the psalms of lament for a while, I first learned about the practice of writing a lament when I was teaching a class at Fuller Seminary. It's an exercise we have our students do as part of a class on vocation. My students found it so helpful that I started to have people do it more broadly in workshops and on retreats. I'd have groups pick a cultural or world issue and then have individuals pick something from their own lives. I have come to realize what a powerful tool it is and how much it can become a channel for being completely honest with God. What I have detailed below comes directly from what we assign students at Fuller.

A psalm of lament has five key parts: *opening address* (who you are talking to), *complaint* (what you're upset about), *con-*

*fession of trust* (telling God where your trust lies), *petition for help* (asking God for help), and *vow of praise* (praising God).

Here's how the structure plays out in Psalm 22:

*Opening address*: My God, my God (v. 1a)

*Complaint*: Why have you forsaken me? Why are you so far from helping me, from the words of my groaning? (v. 1b)

*Confession of trust*: Yet you are holy, enthroned on the praises of Israel. In you our ancestors trusted; they trusted, and you delivered them. To you they cried, and were saved; in you they trusted, and were not put to shame. (vv. 3–5)

*Petition for help*: Do not be far from me, for trouble is near and there is no one to help. (vv. 11, 19b)

*Vow of praise*: From the horns of the wild oxen you have rescued me. I will tell of your name to my brothers and sisters; in the midst of the congregation I will praise you. (vv. 21–22)

I encourage you to write your own psalm of lament about some aspect of your work or life. Try to pick something that has caused you pain or made you feel unsettled. It might help to think about where you feel like you're in the tomb, hoping for resurrection. It might help to think about when your experiences haven't matched your expectations or the ground has shifted beneath you. I encourage you to lament freely to God.

# PART THREE

# How Will You Get There?

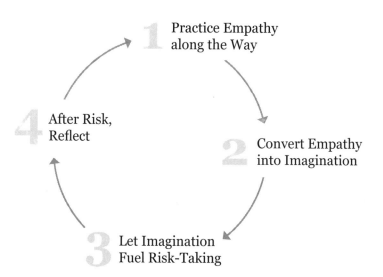

1 Practice Empathy along the Way

2 Convert Empathy into Imagination

3 Let Imagination Fuel Risk-Taking

4 After Risk, Reflect

# 8

# Practice Empathy along the Way

In our Age of Overwhelm, we need tools that help us to not only stay afloat in the raging waters of change but also thrive amid all the chaos. At the heart of these tools is an invitation to recognize, push back on, and reorient the messages that would otherwise seek to tell us we don't have what it takes, or aren't who it takes, to find a meaningful way forward in this changing world.

I'm convinced that so much of our pushing back happens when we make daily choices that over time stack together to form our character and outlook on life. In other words, we are what we do. Consider the woman who complains to her husband every day about her boss and her coworkers. Over time, she finds that bitterness and discouragement have grabbed ahold of her heart. She is less happy than she used to be, and while part of her unhappiness can be blamed on her context, she also senses that her bitterness comes from her daily habit of complaining.

Or consider the not-so-fit man who suffers a heart attack and decides that he will no longer live recklessly with his health. He stops eating fatty foods, cuts way back on alcohol, and takes up running, all with the goal of seeing his grandkids graduate from high school. Over time, he reduces his cholesterol, sleeps better, and doesn't feel so out of breath when he chases his grandkids around the yard. When asked about his transformation, he credits the small, daily choices that had sort of a domino effect on his health and his outlook on life. What we spend our time on is not only an output of our energy. The ways we spend our time are inputs as well. What we do, what we love, who we do life with—they all shape us. Our *doing* shapes our *being*. And then our *being* shapes our *doing*. The actions and rhythms of our lives form what we care about and how we live.

To this end, the next four chapters offer a method for walking the entrepreneurial way in a down-to-earth, daily kind of way: Less about how to start a business and more about how to seize opportunity, create value, and face risk. Less about how to change the entire world and more about how to change how you engage the world. Less about trying to replicate what others are doing and more about trusting that you're creative and resilient and that God has designed you for meaningful relationships. Less about finding the most meaningful, heart-satisfying job and more about how to let God infuse meaning into everything you do.

The method contains four action-oriented principles that get less abstract when they take the shape of practices—

rhythms of *doing* that shape our *being*. These practices are meant to build off one another, which is why they are linked in name and presented as a cycle.

While I've presented these practices in a linear fashion, it's important to name that walking the entrepreneurial way isn't always linear. I trust that as you learn the rhythm of these practices and try them on for size in your life and work, you'll almost certainly recognize situations that catalyze you straight into thinking about your next doable risk or to reflecting with gratitude. So think of these practices both as a set of intentional rhythmic activities you can cultivate and as principles that, as you become more attuned, you'll be able to pull off the shelf, depending on what situation you find yourself in. Again, your *doing* shapes your *being*. What you cultivate behind the scenes in the quiet, private, daily moments in your life and work will come center stage in the bigger moments of your life.

First, *practice empathy along the way.*

I am convinced that our very best and most meaningful work can be traced back to empathy. This is certainly true when it comes to product development and breakthrough inventions. But it's also true in our more ordinary work as humans. Consider the father who teaches his daughter to read because he senses how she delights in stories. Or the executive who institutes family leave for her employees because she remembers how hard it was to go to the office and raise young kids. Or the postal carrier who remembers not only the names of everyone on his route, but also the names of their kids, because he's learned that the quickest way to make someone smile is to ask about the in-between moments in life.

When empathy informs our decision-making at every level, meaning is infused into our work. In a sense, centering empathy captures part of what Luther was arguing for when the Reformers toppled the normative theology of vocation in the 1500s. Though I argued that we leave the notion of static roles behind, there's a part of Luther's framing that feels all the more relevant today. He argued that vocation was a place to love and serve our neighbors. Empathy, then, is the way we listen to our neighbors—the people along the way with us in life—so that we might love them in a way that comes from our knowing and seeing their needs.

In the Age of Overwhelm, this kind of daily empathy might feel a bit counterintuitive.

When the narrative that we are in our own solo ship casts us as the heroes (or potentially failures) in our individual pursuits of success, we can end up making decisions about how to spend our time on a rubric rooted in self-centeredness, preoccupation, and overstimulation: *How could we possibly attend to the needs of one more person? We need people to attend to us! We don't have any bandwidth for others! Hello, we're drowning! We need a lifeboat; we can't be one!* In the Age of Overwhelm, God's call to love and serve our neighbors can feel like one more impossible to-do.

But it's right in the midst of the chaos of life that I'd like to suggest empathy as a subversion tactic in the face of overwhelm—a tool for sacred resistance. Empathy is a way for us as holy noisemakers to declare that we will not be swept up by the rapids, we will not give into the encouragement to make it all about us, we will not hunker down alone in our kayaks. Instead, we will trust that the way forward is together.

We will trust that moving toward others in their pains and hopes alike is not only good for whomever we're moving toward but also really good for us. We will believe in letting empathy calibrate our decision-making and our way forward in work so that we might reject any vision of a life that would become too much about us alone.

## What Is Empathy?

In order to talk about empathy *along the way*, first let's just talk about empathy. Some of you are natural empathizers and therefore don't need me to define *empathy*. You already feel it in your bones. I know you because my daughter is one of you. Once when my kids were playing, I heard my then one-year-old son scream from the other room. Before I knew what was happening, my three-year-old daughter had left my side and was at his. She was a critical millisecond ahead of me, carefully unraveling a shoelace from around his neck. She was completely calm as she helped him out of a scary situation. After consoling him and praising her, I asked her what made her go to him so quickly. She told me, "Mommy, I could feel his scared in my heart." I already knew she was empathetic, but on that day I came to understand that it was her superpower. Empathy in its most basic form was on display that day. Empathy is when we feel someone else's feelings and we're motivated to join them or act on their behalf. Empathy sounds like *I see you, I feel you, I hear you, and I'm with you.*

In my own pursuit of a more nuanced understanding of empathy and how it works, I've found Daniel Goleman's work helpful. Goleman is the psychologist who popularized the concept of emotional intelligence, and one of the things I love about him is his ability to present complex ideas in relatable ways. He breaks empathy down into three categories: *cognitive empathy, social empathy,* and *empathetic concern.*[1]

First is *cognitive empathy,* the ability to imagine someone else's circumstances or feelings. Let's say it's performance-review season at work. One of your closest work friends is often at odds with your boss and is therefore fretting his review. You know your boss isn't satisfied with your friend's work, so you imagine your friend is going to have a hard review with the boss. During the time you know the review is scheduled, you imagine to yourself how it's going. You imagine that your friend is feeling defensive and maybe angry, maybe even sad. This ability to imagine how your friend feels is cognitive empathy.

Next is *social empathy,* the ability to feel with someone in the moment. Let's say that after your friend's performance review, you two go out for lunch. At lunch, he tells you about how much the conversation sucked and how critical your boss was. When he describes the conversation, you wince, feeling his discomfort in that moment. And as he starts to feel discouraged, recounting parts of the conversation, you feel discouraged with him. This is social empathy.

Goleman's last category is *empathetic concern*. This is not just imagining what someone else feels or even feeling it in the moment with them. Rather, you are driven by empathy to some sort of action. Listening to your friend makes you feel so discouraged that you just have to do something about it. Maybe you write a list of ten things you appreciate about their work and give it to them. Maybe you coach them on how to navigate their relationship with your boss. Maybe you even talk to your boss. The point is that you're motivated to action. This is empathetic concern.

Whenever I teach or speak about what empathy is and how I've come to believe in empathy's critical role for work in a changing world, folks come up to me afterward and thank me. Not because they've learned anything new about empathy—in fact, they probably could have taught about empathy with more sophistication and personal experience than I could. They thank me because they feel they've just received validation for their superpower—permission to trust and harness the empathy they so naturally feel and not to shy away from it. One woman described to me that in her experience, while empathy is increasingly talked about in books and on podcasts, it's not as accepted in everyday work situations. She explained that in her twenty years working in small businesses, her empathy was talked about as a girly or touchy-feely trait—a skill that was good for after-hours girl talk but not a valued tool for decision-making in the workplace. We acknowledged that there are of course certain professions that do center empathy—such as counseling, nursing, and teaching. But if you don't find yourself in one of those, and sometimes even if you do, it's not always easy to see the link between empathy and everyday work or to feel that it's a welcomed practice.

What's ironic is that empathy has actually been valued in certain aspects of business for a while. Businesses are almost constantly asking what their customers need and how to market the products they sell to those customers. There is an entire philosophy (and a subsequent set of tools) related to product development called *design thinking*. Design thinking is about understanding and designing for human needs as a strategy for creating viable and meaningful products. Design thinking methods have been adopted widely across industries—from start-ups trying to deliver new technology to social enterprises trying to solve big problems to school children trying to serve their neighborhoods. How do we understand human needs? Through empathy.

If empathy is so widely valued in certain aspects of business and is indeed perceived central to certain professions, why can it still feel as though we as individuals can't bring our empathy to work? Why the disconnect?

How do we harness empathy to infuse meaning into our everyday work? How might we let the needs and hopes, fears and joys of others motivate us to seize opportunity, create value, and face risk? At the same time, how do we not let the feelings of others overwhelm us in such a way that we are paralyzed and unable to engage wholeheartedly? Plus, what about those of us who don't have empathy as a superpower (hello, me!)? How can we grow in our empathetic capacities, our attunement to other people's needs?

I want to suggest that whatever role empathy currently plays in our lives and work, each of us can benefit from a rather ordinary approach to empathy: practicing it *along the way*.

## What Is Empathy *along the Way*?

Whenever you read the phrase *along the way* in this chapter, picture a road. Maybe it's the same road of calling that you drew in chapter 4 (if you haven't done that exercise yet, it really is incredible!). Or maybe it's a real-life road from a place you love. You might imagine a dirt road flanked by redwoods or a sandy path next to water. Whatever your road looks like, consider it as a metaphor for the path you've traveled so far in life. The moment we come into the world, we're all en route from some sort of point *a* to point *z*. Along the way, we're subject to the ebbs and flows and the highs and lows of being a soul formed in motion. We're subject to the day-by-day, on-the-way realities of work and love that happen as life unfolds. And of course, so much of our road is marked by relationships—the people we trust and love deeply, folks we work with or go to school with, friends and family from our wider circle. People we admire and even those who have hurt us. Strangers. Loved ones. All the people we meet along the way are part of our road. On this road and with these people, we are best poised to practice empathy in an everyday sort of way.

When I think about empathy along the way, I think about Jesus's parable of the good Samaritan in Luke 10. It's a classic example of how the power of empathy can be so captivating, causing us to detour from our routes and plans in the most sacred way possible. In this story, there's an expert in the law who interrupts Jesus to ask about what one must do to inherit eternal life. While the lawyer's tone is almost impossible to discern, the public context in which this story takes place leads me to believe that he is challenging Jesus. Put bluntly, the lawyer feels rude, snarky, and a bit self-centered.

Jesus responds to the lawyer's question with his own question, asking him what the Torah says about eternal life.

The lawyer recites the well-known text: "Love the Lord your God with all your heart and with all your soul and with all your strength and with all your mind," and "Love your neighbor as yourself" (vv. 27, 29). Jesus acknowledges the man's response as a sufficient one. But the expert, who is seeking to justify himself, prods further: "And who is my neighbor?"

It's important to call out the lawyer's motivation here. His questions don't seem to be driven by empathy or by love or by service to the neighbor he is able to name as important. No, his motivation is to justify himself. He's self-centered at best, selfish at worst. He continues to interrupt Jesus and center his own needs.

Truthfully, I can identify with this interrupting lawyer who wants to justify himself. I can identify with being so preoccupied with my own security that I fail to grasp what God is trying to teach me. I can't help but wonder about the lawyer: Was he anxious? Was he lonely? Was he exhausted and overwhelmed?

Next, Jesus turns the lawyer's mental model of what it means to be a neighbor completely upside down by telling a story that highlights the stark contrast between social elites, who do not take the time to move toward someone in need, and a Samaritan—moved by compassion to cross the road in loving service of his neighbor.

If you're familiar with the story, you know that Jesus first describes a traveler who was robbed, attacked, and left for dead. Then, good news! A priest sees him. But wait, he doesn't stop. Instead, he moves away from the man in need. But don't worry . . . here comes a Levite! Surely, he'll help. But he too moves to the other side of the road, leaving the man behind. Finally, an unlikely hero—a Samaritan—makes his way down the road and sees the man. Driven by merciful compassion, the Samaritan physically moves toward the hurt traveler, attending to his wounds, placing the vulnerable man on his own donkey, and walking him into town. He finds a place for him to heal, and makes a deal with an innkeeper to cover the costs for watching after the man while he recovers.

There's so much here to unpack. The first two individuals to pass by the injured traveler were a Levite and a priest. Based on these one-word descriptions, we can assume that probably, unlike the Samaritan, these two men held prominent places in the sociocultural hierarchy of the time, kind of like the lawyer. Yet they are not the exemplars of neighborly love. They are not willing to be interrupted by empathy. The Samaritan is. Why didn't the priest and the Levite help the hurt man? Were they too afraid? Overwhelmed? Focused on their own way forward? Concerned with their own to-dos? Did they lack compassion and imagination for their neighbor?

No matter the case, Jesus's story invites us to consider that exemplars in empathy—people to model our behavior after—are perhaps not found at the center of organizations or at the top of the social ladder. Additionally, all four of these men were travelers presumably en route from some sort of point *a* to point *b*. The first man was attacked along the way. The priest and the Levite moved away from the hurt man and instead continued along the way to wherever they were going. But the Samaritan *practiced empathy along the way.*

I don't know if the Samaritan had empathy as his superpower or if he had to work to cultivate his empathetic muscles and his capacity to act on compassion. Either way, he was able to let empathy interrupt him along the way to wherever he was going. He was able to make a series of decisions about using his resources—his oil, donkey, time, money—in pursuit of joining this man in his moment of need. Plus, he was willing to face risk because he slowed his journey on an already dangerous road and he entered into an open-ended financial contract with an innkeeper who might exploit him. Yet he did it anyway. Driven by empathy, he subverted all the shoulds and should nots. It was the Samaritan, the one who was driven by empathy to join his neighbor, who was lifted up that day by Jesus as the exemplar for the lawyer.

So then, how do we let this story of empathy-driven action, of a holy and interruptible posture, guide our expectations about who to listen to, tend to, and join on an everyday basis? We may encounter someone on the side of the road left for dead in our daily work. What does practicing empathy along the way look like in our work?

One of my favorite stories of practicing empathy along the way (and eventually exercising imagination, risk-taking, and reflection too) is in the story of how the nonprofit Kiva was founded.

Jessica Jackley is the cofounder of Kiva, a microfinancing organization that "envisions a financially inclusive world where all people hold the power to improve their lives."[2] When we talked, I was struck by the role empathy played in how Kiva began. Jessica was in Africa, working with another development organization. While there, she met "entrepreneur after entrepreneur who were each doing amazing things with very small amounts of money."[3] For Jessica, their stories stood in stark contrast to the more common narrative coming out of Western fundraising work. Many of those efforts are about catalyzing compassion with stories of desperation and sadness. And to be fair, that method did elicit a particular kind of empathy. But those stories just didn't match the people Jessica was actually meeting. These folks—these entrepreneurs—were overflowing with creativity and energy. Jessica reflected with me,

> Pretty naively, I started to ask some basic questions like, Well, gosh, what if I stayed in touch with these new friends? What if I shared these different stories, these entrepreneurial stories, these business-centric stories of success with my friends and family as opposed to these stories of sadness and suffering and desperation and hopelessness to get them to donate? What if instead it was, "Hey, here's a person working hard, boot-strapping it, lifting themselves out of poverty. They just need a loan." Wouldn't that be an interesting kind of social experiment to attempt?[4]

I have no idea if empathy comes naturally to Jessica or if she has to work at it. But what I can say is this: she was able to set aside the narrative she was supposed to buy into and hear the folks she met on their terms. Ultimately, I think this is what enabled her to witness up close the beautiful, honorable qualities of their work. She was able to recognize joy as such because she was open to another narrative than the one so often told. And she bet on the fact that others would be drawn to these stories just as she was. I see this as a second layer of empathy—this feeling that it might be motivating to potential lenders to invest in a potentially sustainable business that could have potentially powerful communal ripple effects. It worked. To date, Kiva has facilitated over $1.4 billion in loans to entrepreneurs around the world. Many of these loans are for as little as $25.

What I love about Jessica's story is that she didn't go out of her way to formally practice listening or empathy. She didn't set up a listening session or send out a survey in an email. Instead, she was attuned to the environment she was in. She practiced empathy *along the way.*

One time in a workshop, I asked attendees to make a list of people with whom they were already on the way in their lives and work. As I surveyed the room to see how people were doing with the prompt, most seemed to have no problem writing out a list of people they engaged with regularly or semiregularly. But one woman was just sitting there, pen in hand, staring blankly at her paper. I walked over to her and asked her how it was going.

In a quiet room full of people doing their work, she burst into loud tears and said, "I don't have anyone. I'm all alone. I'm not married, I recently left my job, and my family all lives on another continent." After we had a good, long hug and took a few deep breaths, I asked her about her daily rhythms. Where did she grocery stop? Did she take walks around her neighborhood? Whose names were in her email inbox and who were her last several text messages from? Before long, she had a list, actually a long list. Afterward we talked and she named that although she felt incredibly isolated and lonely, people weren't actually that far away.

Consider whom you already interact with along the way in your work and in the rest of life—your teammates, your boss, your employees, your customers or clients, your patients or your students, your kids or your friends. The person you see at church or the barista at your local coffee shop, your kid's teacher or the neighbor next door. Think for a moment about the people you engage with on a daily, weekly, and monthly basis.

## Love Your Neighbor AND Yourself

For every bit of conviction I have for letting empathy interrupt, loving your neighbor along the way, and making decisions rooted in your moving toward others, we've also got to talk about the *yourself* part in "love your neighbor as yourself." You cannot move toward others in a healthy, wholehearted, and helpful way if you are not committed to moving toward yourself.

I learned just how holy and critical the move toward ourselves is a few years ago when I was developing a six-part process that helps people make sense of the season of work they're in and discern the next steps on their road ahead. The process mirrors much of this book and draws on the four-step formation method presented in these last chapters: practice empathy along the way, convert empathy into imagination, let imagination fuel risk-taking, and reflect with

189

gratitude. Early in beta testing our process, my team and I hit a wall on how to facilitate the session on empathy. I had designed the experience with the intention of helping people name their own vocational pain and then practice moving toward other people as a means to widen their imagination about what God might be up to within them.

In the first group I led, I remember choosing my words carefully to usher folks into an exercise that asked them to design their own experiment in empathy—something tangible they could do the next week that would help them lean into their own vocational pain. I gave everyone ten minutes to brainstorm alone and then called the group back to share. I still remember most of the ideas people came up with: walks in the woods, coffee with themselves, deep breaths and prayer, saying no to external pressures, saying yes to themselves, trusting that they were enough. Their ideas were compassionate and grounded, and you could feel that what each of them had decided to do was infused with a lot of meaning. There was just one problem: nearly all of what people wanted to do didn't involve other people. Almost every idea was something that helped people move toward themselves. I thought about trying to course correct, but people were so emotional and so excited about what they planned to do that my instincts told me to just let it be. I chalked it up to my poor explanation and thought, *Oh well, I'll do a better job next time.*

In the next cohort of folks when we got to the empathy session, I worked even harder on my delivery and was really explicit about the fact that empathy was about others, not about ourselves. Yet we got the same results. At the time, we had two other group leaders running their own beta

190

groups. Guess what? They also got the same results. When we sat down to figure out what was going on, one of my brilliant teammates helped me see that participants were revealing gaps in our process, and that it was good news. If we used this as an opportunity to build around where they wanted to go, we could design something even more helpful. So we let their revelations on empathy interrupt the prescribed route for where we thought the groups should go. We moved toward our participants and built around their instincts, not ours.

By listening to the groups, I've learned that one of the most critical steps in dealing with pain and eventually cultivating the muscles to move toward others is self-compassion. We must love both our neighbor and ourselves. And sometimes it's far too easy to miss the loving ourselves part.

Extending empathy toward others requires us to make peace with our own pain. Father Richard Rohr says, "*If we do not transform our pain, we will most assuredly transmit it*—usually to those closest to us: our family, our neighbors, our co-workers, and, invariably, the most vulnerable, our children."[5]

What I realize now that felt so mysterious to me when I first designed those groups is that the move toward others requires us to travel *through* our own pain. In order to empathize with what someone else is going through, we've got to trust the process of tapping into those same feelings in our own experiences. Moving toward ourselves—and loving what we find—is rooted in our trust that God meets us in our mess.

Hebrews 4 says, "For we do not have a high priest who is unable to empathize with our weakness, but we have one who has been tempted in every way, just as we are—yet he did not sin. Let us then approach God's throne of grace with confidence, so that we may receive mercy and find grace to help us in our time of need" (vv. 15–16).

God knows intimately what it is to be human. Jesus empathizes with the pain and suffering of it all. And right there, right in the midst of the worst of the worst, we are welcomed to draw near to the throne of God. We are welcomed to come and receive grace in our time of need. Remember, resilience is a gift of resurrection.

Of course the people in our groups sensed they needed to approach the throne of grace. Of course they wanted to carve out some time to care for themselves as an act of mercy. Of course they wisely sensed that any empathetic concern they might extend to someone else would come from knowing they are loved and held by God and serve a God who first empathizes with us.

These groups have taught me so much about the sacred work of listening not only to others but also to our own souls *along the way*. Our souls crave the space to be quiet and deal with what they must, all at the foot of the Holy One who leans in and listens with a tender ear of compassion. In this, we are reminded that the one who calls our name and beckons us on the way forward is the same one who listens to us along the way.

### EXERCISE: Move toward Someone

To move toward someone this week, complete the following steps:

1. Spend five minutes making a list of specific people you currently encounter along the way. These should be people with whom you have some sort of regular interaction. Regular could be monthly, weekly, or daily. Think about your colleagues, family members, friends, people in your neighborhood, and so on. Include yourself on the list. Most people are surprised by how many people they end up having on their list.

2. Slowly read back through your list, noticing which names seem to stand out. Maybe when you see them they jump off the page or you feel yourself stir a bit.

3. Circle the names that stand out. Maybe you circled three names. Maybe you circled five. Maybe you circled yourself; maybe you didn't.

4. Narrow the names you've circled to one or two people you want to move toward *this week*. You may choose more than two, especially if you feel compelled to move toward yourself. What exactly do we mean by *move toward*? We mean that you take the emotional posture of the Samaritan in that you tune in to their needs and feelings and circumstances in an especially attentive way.

5. After you've selected your one or two people, set an alarm on your phone or an event in your calendar for exactly one week from now. When that alarm goes off or that event comes up, take fifteen minutes to reflect in your journal on the following questions:

   a. What happened when you moved toward your person?

b. How did what you heard in them speak back into your own sense of learning and longing and discovery in this season?

c. What got in the way of you moving toward your person?

d. What new questions do you have?

# Convert Empathy into Imagination

The last chapter was about *practicing empathy along the way*—letting the daily act of noticing others interrupt our work and our lives. But after we move toward others, what do we do next? What happens after we listen long enough that we are able to truly see the needs and hopes of others? Guided by the big story that bonds us and the Spirit who leads us, we can *convert the empathy we feel into imagination* about how to join in with what God is doing.

The act of imagining is as simple and as stunning as the act of picturing what we cannot see. Whenever we let ourselves picture possibility, we are engaged in a holy act.

Why holy? For me, our human capacity to imagine is one of the great gifts of being made in the image of a creative

God. If creativity is about bridging the gap between reality and possibility, imagination is the place of possibility. It's what guides our steps forward.

The hard part is that converting our noticing of people into ideas about how to join God and join people along the way isn't exactly a technical conversion. It's not quite like when a bank converts dollars into euros or a driver converts kilometers into miles. Those conversions have mathematical formulas that undergird them. But we don't have a technical formula for converting empathy into imagination. Plus, it can sometimes get problematic fast if we try to come up with solutions for people's problems all on our own. We're not the Savior, after all.

Let's consider an example of what this conversion of empathy into imagination looks like played out. Jason is a pastor I know who considers himself to have naturally low levels of both empathy and imagination. He describes himself as great with budgets and deadlines and planning, which make him well-suited for his executive pastor role. Recently, he was telling me about a new budget system he was testing for his team and how the shift in systems was making him feel a bit stressed and a bit excited. I asked him why he decided to switch systems. It turns out that the old system was causing a lot of frustrating extra work for people on his team because it was confusing. Jason told me that after hearing enough of his teammates grumble, he started to have ideas about how he could build something that would help people feel more efficient and less frustrated. For the record, the old system never bothered him. But it did frustrate him to be administering a system that felt inefficient for others and that just ended up wasting organizational resources and putting people in bad moods, which seemed bad for morale.

Jason sensed brokenness in his team's budgeting system by listening to the frustrations of his colleagues. That's *practicing empathy along the way.* Then he imagined ways to create a system that stewarded people's time better. That's *converting empathy to imagination.* Testing the new system was his *next doable risk*—a move we'll talk about more in the next chapter. For now, let's turn to thinking about what should guide us as we seek to imagine possibilities for the way forward.

**Redemption Is Our Compass**

As followers of Christ, we have particular responsibilities and opportunities when it comes to converting empathy into imagination. We are guided by a story of redemption and an active Spirit at work in the world. *We are called to follow Jesus by creatively working, especially toward God's mission of redemption in the world, through particular relationships, roles, places, tasks, and moments.*

God's callings to us are always layered—kind of like the nesting dolls we considered in chapter 3. The innermost doll is the call to belong to Jesus. The second doll is God's call to participate in God's redemptive mission in the world. The third doll is God's call to creatively work toward that mission. The outermost doll is God's call to particulars— relationships, roles, places, tasks, and moments—in loving service to the people of God and the world God loves.

Put another way, redemption is our compass for imagination. Let's unpack this a bit. You may have guessed by now that the book of Luke is my favorite book of the Bible. I love how this Gospel writer portrays Jesus as unabashedly *for* the outsider. I love how he portrays Jesus as turning upside down the rules of society. Jesus welcomes and is for everyone. Plus, there are many stories in which we see the move from empathy to imagination.

Luke 5 contains one of them. We learn that Jesus is teaching. Everyone has come to hear Jesus and be healed by him that day. We read that a man who can't walk is trying to get to Jesus. He's lying on a mat, carried by some friends. The men do their best to get through the crowd but aren't able to do so. There aren't many details in the text, but I can just picture the man pleading with his friends to get him to Jesus. Or maybe it was one of the friends' ideas. Whatever the case, they decide to take the man up to the roof and get him in that way. Can't you just imagine one of them saying, "What if we got up onto the roof of the house and lowered him in? We could get him right in front of the healer! Jesus would have to heal him then!"

The friends practiced empathy on the way as they leaned into the needs of their friend on the mat. And they converted that empathy into imagination when they decided to try to get him in front of Jesus by going in through the roof. Then, they let that imagination fuel risk by actually acting on the idea. (We'll talk more about risk in the next chapter.)

When the friends lowered the man down into the house, the text says, "When Jesus saw *their* faith," he said to the paralyzed man, "Friend, your sins are forgiven" (v. 20, emphasis added). Until this point in the day, Jesus had presumably been healing people from physical ailments. That's probably why the man and his friends were so desperate to get through the crowd. But now, in a plot twist, Jesus forgives this man's sins. Importantly, the man isn't yet able to get up and walk, making it clear that Jesus doesn't link together his paralysis and his sins.

But some of the folks gathered didn't like that Jesus was claiming he could forgive sins. That was blasphemy! In response to their questions, Jesus challenged them about the limits of their own imaginations. Sure, physical healing was good and wonderful and indeed miraculous—a gift from God. But God's greatest gift to humanity was forgiveness of sins and eternal life through the life, death, and resurrection of Jesus.

It's often the case that our imaginations are a bit limited about what God might do, that our compasses aren't completely pointed toward what Jesus means by redemption. I suppose this is why we must be open to letting God continually widen our imaginations about the many, many ways redemption takes place in our everyday lives. Sometimes, like the folks in that house in Jesus's day, we're set in our ways about what we think goodness and truth look like. But there Jesus is, right in the midst of our certainty—inviting us to widen our imaginations and dial our compasses in toward redemption.

Rachel Goble is the founder of the Freedom Story, an organization that works to end human trafficking through preventative education. The mission of Freedom Story is in obvious alignment with God's priority of redemption. But as we talked, I was inspired by how the mission of redemption permeated everything the organization does.

Rachel told me how the very first student who graduated from Freedom Story's trafficking prevention program helped her to "reimagine how to imagine."[1] Rachel explained that she was talking with this woman and asked her how she felt about the way the organization had told her story to prospective donors. The woman shared honestly with Rachel that she had come a long way from who that girl was, that she was in a different season of her life and wanted to be remembered for who she is today—not just who she was back then.[2]

It made sense to Rachel that the woman wished to be known by who she is, not by who she was, that she wanted to be known by the arc of redemption rather than let setback or struggle have the final word. That interaction helped Rachel and Freedom Story reimagine how they told stories. The language they now use is *ethical storytelling*. The point of ethical storytelling is that every story told is to be charitable to the people in the story—especially when imagining their future selves. When I think about this shift at Freedom Story, I can't help but see the contrast between telling stories that focus on where we are and telling stories that help shape our imagination about where we might go.

Rachel was willing to let the organizational practice of storytelling be redeemed to more honestly reflect the arc of redemption in their work and in people's lives. Rachel was willing to reimagine. She was open to deeper and fuller ways for redemption to play out through the work of the Freedom Story.

### Ask *What If?*

If empathy sounds like *I see you, I feel you, I hear you, and I'm with you*, then imagination sounds like *What if?* When our hearts and minds are calibrated to God's mission of redemption in the world, our what-if questions can yield possibilities worth putting our energy into.

Remember Jessica Jackley and Kiva? When Jessica met business-minded entrepreneurs who stood in contrast to the more typical development stories, she was drawn in. Remember what she said to me:

> Pretty naively, I started to ask some basic questions like, "Well, gosh, *what if* I stayed in touch with these new friends? *What if* I shared these different stories, these entrepreneurial stories, these business-centric stories of success with my friends and family as opposed to these stories of sadness and suffering and desperation and hopelessness to get them to donate?" *What if* instead it was, "Hey, here's a person working hard, boot-strapping it, lifting themselves out of poverty. They just need a loan." Wouldn't that be an interesting kind of social experiment to attempt?[3]

In asking *what if?* Jessica took the next step. She converted empathy into imagination. She imagined how she could use her resources to help connect would-be investors with promising entrepreneurs. This is why even though converting empathy into imagination might sound a bit abstract, over time I've noticed just how down-to-earth and utterly human the move is.

Or take the good Samaritan. When Luke introduces him, he says, "But a Samaritan, as he traveled, came where the man was; and when he saw him, he took pity on him. He went to him and bandaged his wounds, pouring on oil and wine. Then he put the man on his own donkey, brought him to an inn and took care of him" (Luke 10:33–34).

We do not hear the Samaritan ask, "What if?" in the text. We don't see God break in from on high to give the Samaritan imagination about what he might do. Yet the Samaritan seems to rush to the man in need. He tends to him. He takes him on as a fellow traveler. As I've spent time with this text, I have wondered about what might have been going through the Samaritan's head. In the parable that Jesus tells, I have come to think of the space between verses 33 and 34 kind of like a holy chasm. A little, itty-bitty break in the text in which I have to believe the Samaritan walked toward the man and simultaneously wondered, *Should I?* or *But what if I?* or *How can I not?*

If I were going to rewrite this story to really draw out how it sounds when we convert empathy into imagination, it might go something like this: "But a Samaritan, as he traveled, came to where the man was; and when he saw him, he took pity on him. *And before he knew what his feet were doing, he was walking toward the hurt man, wondering, What if I took this man with me? Can I do that? Will we both be in danger? Will he slow me down? What if I don't go to him? What if I just leave him? What will happen to him? No, that won't be good. Yes, okay, there's only one right thing to do.* He went to him and bandaged his wounds, pouring on oil and wine. Then he put the man on his own donkey, brought him to an inn, and *commissioned an innkeeper to take care of the wounded man.*"

What I love about this story is that there's no way the good Samaritan had it all figured out right away. There's no way he could imagine the entire big picture or the rest of the journey. More likely, his imagination about next steps grew from the choices he made along the way: *What if I go to this man? Okay, I bandaged his wounds, now what? What if I take him into town? Okay, we're in town, now what? What if I pay an innkeeper to look after him?*

In addition to the what-if questions potentially running through the Samaritan's head, Jesus is doing such an interesting thing with this passage. As is so often the case, Jesus uses a story to widen the imagination of anyone listening. In this, it seems that Jesus's goal is to help us know what true north really looks like. It's as if Jesus is saying, "Oh, you think the path to eternal life is well-worn and formulaic? Actually the path to eternal life is about so much more." Or to the folks in the house in Luke 5, Jesus might have said, "You think physical healing is the greatest thing? Actually, the greatest thing is the forgiveness of sin."

## Immerse Yourself in Stories

If Jesus is such a lover of stories and if he uses them time and time again to reshape, widen, and point our imaginations toward redemption, then stories are a serious part of the way forward. Let me be super up-front that I am very biased when it comes to how stories can widen our imagination about what's possible. In my time as a creative producer, I have sat with hundreds of people and listened to how stories shaped what they think the future can hold. How stories introduced them to a new culture or idea or helped them change their mind on politics or religion.

I had my own immersion into the power of story when, in 2007 as a twenty-four-year-old, I moved to Hawaii to run away from a bad breakup with a man I thought I was going to marry—not because God was redeeming my love life but rather because I took a job as a middle school Bible teacher on the island of Oahu. As part of my duties in a small school, I oversaw seventh grade homeroom. Homeroom was twenty minutes of to-dos at the end of the day. I hated that feeling of trying to get kids to clean, so I did the only natural thing: I bribed them. The deal was that if they finished all the chair stacking and sweeping and desk arranging within five minutes (all it really should have taken anyway), we would have story time for the remainder of homeroom.

I started by telling whatever stories I could think of—captivating them with silly stories from my teenage years and tales about my big Irish Catholic family. But I ran out of stories fast! Finally, it dawned on me to have the kids tell stories.

I heard about things I never otherwise would have during story time. One girl told us about when someone tried to sell her drugs on the beach. A boy told us about how his dad had been gone on a work trip for two months. One girl always told stories about make-believe cats. From those kids, I heard stories that made me laugh and stories that made me cry.

The stories certainly gave me empathy for all that kids face on a daily basis. And over time, that empathy gave way to imagination. As I listened closely, I'd notice the patterns of what was happening and then develop our curriculum around whatever was going on in their lives. When I heard stories of how hard it was to feel like they didn't fit in, I thought, *What if we did an entire series on the awesomeness of biblical misfits?* When I heard about how hard it was to use their voice, I thought, *What if together we mined the stories of Esther and Moses to cultivate looking for models of bravery in these kids?* Plus, beyond those curriculum ideas, I was able to just be an empathetic adult who met them in their pain, their longings, and their hopes. Most of the time, I was able to honestly say, "Hey, I've been there before." Of all the lessons I planned and the work I did that year at that school, those fifteen minutes were by far the most helpful and meaningful.

Why are stories so powerful? Why do we remember them and watch them, tell them and sometimes try to forget them? It's because stories hold people; they are naturally both safe and challenging. Safe because when there's something about a character—real or fictional—that sparks our sense of empathy or mirrors our own story, we're in. But challenging if there's something that feels different from what we're used to or in regard to our values. It's this mix of safety and challenge that makes stories something that can widen our imaginations and influence our behaviors.

Jesus's use of stories highlights that they shape our sense of self and sense of community. Researcher Margaret Somers says,

> People construct identities (however multiple and changing) by locating themselves or being located within a repertoire of emplotted stories; that "experience" is constituted through narratives; that people make sense of what has happened and is happening to them by attempting to assemble or in some way to integrate these happenings within one or more narratives.[4]

Somers's point is that we journey through life connecting with and ultimately locating ourselves within a variety of stories. Consider the stories you listen to that shape your imagination. Consider the people you listen to and learn from—and consider those who might be outside your current purview. Consider how the patterns of redemption play out—or don't—in these stories. Consider how the stories you're immersed in shape your sense of what's possible, how they shape your capacity to ask redemptive what-if questions.

There is a sign that greets me when I drive into my hometown. Perched high on a bridge that spans the Missouri River, the sign is the color of summer grass with chalk-white letters. It reads, "Nebraska . . . the Good Life." I must have crossed over that bridge a thousand times as a kid, so the words are imprinted on my mind forever. Over time, that slogan—meant to welcome newcomers into the city where I grew up—has become sort of a visual cue for one of my deepest convictions about making meaning in a changing world.

Let me try to explain. Each of us carries with us an internal picture of what we think the world should look like—even if it's buried down deep in our subconscious. Our internal picture illuminates our sense of everything. It guides what makes us happy and what gives us hope. It dictates what we think is just and how we deal with sorrow. Our vision of the good life informs what kind of work we think is meaningful and what kind of jobs we go for. That same vision informs how we shop, where we choose to live, and how we talk to our partners and kids. Our vision of the good life comes with a set of rules. Sometimes these rules are grounding and good. Other times they're limiting and incomplete. Sometimes we're aware of the rules that govern our pursuit of the good life; other times the messages playing in our head are a bit subtler: Be nice. Try hard. Take care of the environment.

The ends justify the means. Some people are born leaders; others are not. You can be good at anything if you try hard enough. Only some people get to have it all. Color within the lines. Break all the rules. Let everyone in. Protect yourself. Cross the road for strangers. Don't get distracted.

Our vision of the good life is our internal compass for how we move through the world. Underneath nearly every decision we make, it's there. My adult life has been about many things, but centrally it's about uncovering the forces that have shaped my innermost vision of the good life and working to reconcile those things with what I've come to believe is God's mission in the world. In other words, I've had to actively let God reshape my imagination. This has meant trading out the parts of my vision of the good life that are limiting or incomplete—and quite frankly don't reflect the mission of God—for a deeper vision of what God's redemption in the world looks like.

### EXERCISE: Ask *What If?*

The goal of this exercise is to notice where imagination comes naturally to you and where you have to work at it. Journal or reflect on the following questions:

1. Where did you imagine or notice imagination in others this week? (It might be helpful to think about when you noticed possibilities, brainstormed, felt a spark of hope, or saw the patterns of redemption play out.)

2. When were you especially excited to ask what-if questions?

3. When did you feel yourself hold back from asking what-if questions?

4. Of all the things you noticed, which of them might God be asking you to pursue and which do you sense are not yours to respond to?

# Take the Next Doable Risks

We've oriented our compasses toward redemption and imagined *what if?* Now it's time to let that imagination—which came on the heels of empathy—fuel risk-taking.

When we think about risks, we tend to imagine the big, hairy, scary choices that can either make or break us. Moving to a new city where you don't know anyone. Quitting a job you love to work at a new place you hope will advance your career. Taking out a loan to start a new business. Going back to school to change career paths. Getting married. Back in Nebraska, we call these "bet the farm" kind of risks, those where both the potential and the cost make you feel as if you're all in.

While it's certainly true that sometimes life invites us to bet the farm and take big risks, most of our daily lives don't play out in such grand fashion. Consider the risks that present themselves to you on a regular basis. You might change course on a project you're working on or increase your prices next time you pitch a job. You might decide to speak up against the majority in a meeting or ask someone you admire to have coffee so you can ask them for advice.

I have found it helpful to think about these daily, weekly, and more rhythmic choices we make as *next doable risks*. A next doable risk is still a risk in that it requires us to make a choice that has an unknown outcome. In chapter 4, I suggested that pursuing opportunity to create value in the face of risk is at the heart of what it means to walk the entrepreneurial way. The other thing worth noting about next doable risks is that I see them as risks that are doable in the present or near term, which means that you likely already have the resources—money, relationships, skills—to take that chance.

Important for the process I'm unfolding in these last chapters is that our risks are rooted in something. Imagining what's possible as we practice empathy along the way fuels our next doable risks. If it helps to think about it linearly: first empathy, then imagination, now risk. This is a sequence that the entrepreneurs I research seem to move through almost intuitively.

We've already seen how this sequence played out in the story of Jessica Jackley and Kiva. We know that when Jessica started Kiva she did so by gathering entrepreneurs' pictures and stories, which she then shared via email with her contact list in hopes of facilitating loans. There were no large investors. There was no impressive technological platform. There was no ten-year plan. There was a camera, a keyboard, and a contact list. Jessica was taking a doable risk with the resources she already had. She was doing something she could actually do. She didn't wait to get started until she had the resources to get going on a grander scale. And perhaps most importantly, the risk she took—and invited others to take with her—was fueled by an imagination about dignifying resource sharing that stemmed from her moving toward people along the way of her present journey.

If empathy sounds like *I see you, I feel you, I hear you, and I'm with you,* and imagination sounds like *what if?* I have come to recognize that risk-taking sounds a lot like *let's try.* Our let's trys can take all kinds of shapes—from a conversation to testing a new budgeting system (remember Jason?) to prototyping a product or service. Jessica's next doable risk—her let's try—was just this, a prototype.

A prototype is a small, testable version of an idea. In a range of fields, designers use prototyping to move ideas from their heads into the physical world. This is used in design thinking. Stanford has been a leader in this field. There you will find the next generation of innovators in lab-like classrooms, working hard to solve humanity's biggest problems with design thinking. You will also find there Dave Evans and Bill Burnett, two professors who teach students how to apply the principles of design thinking—not in order to design the world's best new products but to design their individual lives. Evans and Burnett suggest that people interview seasoned professionals in roles that seem interesting, shadow individuals as they do their jobs, do an internship, or even take on a one-week unpaid project.[1] Through these exercises, people are able to get hands-on experience, try career paths on for size in the smallest of ways, and then reflect on what seemed interesting and appealing and what didn't.

Whether you're pursuing an idea as Jackley did or your individual career path as Evans and Burnett suggest, prototyping can be a concrete way to think about taking your next doable risk.

But what if your next doable risk doesn't feel as concrete? What if it's hard to know exactly what you should do? When I coach or lead groups through this material, I encourage people to take doable risks that are linked to whatever work in empathy and imagination they've just done. Just as I suggest here, I say to those groups that the next doable risk must be fueled by imagination, which is the result of empathetically moving toward people. And when it's still really hard to figure out what to do, I encourage these groups—and you—to think about something that can be done in a relatively short amount of time. Considering what risk you might take within the next week often limits your options in a helpful way.

Whenever I teach the process of moving from empathy to imagination to risk to reflection, I can count on a person or two chiming in when we get to the session on risk. Their confession goes something like this: "I'm not really a risk-taker." Or "I'm not good at risk." Or "Risk is just too scary."

This was Rita. When I first met Rita, her work as an immigration lawyer in Boston had just come to an abrupt halt because of COVID-19. Her husband was in Montreal, and she tried to make her way to him only to learn that the border was temporarily closed. Unable to leave the States and unable to get a new job, she felt isolated and unsure about what to do next. On the recommendation of a friend, she joined me in a cohort where the goal of every member in the group was to discern next steps in our work. We used the four movements presented in this book: empathy, imagination, risk, and reflection.

When we got to the session on risk-taking, I asked everyone if risk was something that came naturally to them or if they had to work at it. Rita was emphatic that risk did not come naturally to her. She just wasn't a born risk-taker.

Then our group read together the good Samaritan passage. We asked ourselves where we noticed risk as we read the text. We talked about how risky it must have been for the Samaritan to slow down his trip. Would he get robbed or beaten? Was he making himself more vulnerable? We wondered together about the level of risk the lawyer took when he interrupted Jesus. We wondered how risky Jesus's upside-down portrayal of the kingdom felt to those who were listening. We remarked on how crazy it felt for the Samaritan to enter into an open-ended financial relationship with an innkeeper he didn't know for the sake of a stranger.

That's when Rita had an aha moment. That's when she realized that her job pushed her into risk every single day. As an immigration lawyer, every day she met people in their pain and worked out plans to help them feel safe and secure. That's when she realized that every time she chooses to move toward someone in empathy and then imagine with them what might be, she is taking a risk. And when framed that way, Rita found herself saying that she was actually quite the risk-taker.

If you think you're not a natural risk-taker, reconsider what it means to take a risk. If you have ever truly practiced empathy, you have already taken a risk. If you have ever looked someone in the face and let their joy spark your joy or their sorrow bring you to your knees, you have already risked so much. You have risked the kind of closeness that yields unpredictable, uncontrollable, human outcomes. And if you've ever let yourself dream, if you've ever let yourself linger on the question *what if?*—then you've already taken a risk, because you've let yourself hope.

When we let ourselves hope for what we cannot see, we risk disappointment and loss. So when we decide to take a chance—to hope anyway, to love anyway, to try anyway—we are taking critical kinds of risks.

I am always amazed at what people in the groups decide to do for their next doable risk and how labeling whatever they did as a risk can be the most liberating part of it. One man decided to write—a muscle he hadn't flexed in a long time because he was frightened at what might come out. One woman decided to ask a colleague she had long admired but had been nervous to approach to collaborate on an upcoming project. Another man decided he'd ask a friend to do some goal setting with him. Sometimes our next doable risk is one that propels us immediately forward, while other times it helps us slow down or even circle back to something that needs tending.

This was the case for Jenn. She entered into our group, having just closed her business and, in a fog, wondering about her next career steps. In the very first group session, I say to people the same thing I said to you at the top of this book: "You are here to do the work you need to do."

Jenn did figure out her next career steps, but she quickly realized that going forward would only be possible if she resolved the pain of the past. Jenn shared with us that one of the reasons she'd closed her business was that she had a painful falling out with her business partner. They had said some awful things to each other. Fueled by her imagination that God might want to restore this friendship, Jenn decided that she'd take a risk and reach out for a conversation with her former partner.

When we met back up at the next session, I was eager to hear how that talk went. Jenn reported to us that her friend did text her back but that she wasn't ready to sit down and talk. So Jenn decided to write a letter to her friend that she would never send—just to name her feelings and start to grieve so that she could ultimately start to move forward.

What I appreciate about Jenn's story is that it didn't have a quick resolution. Her former partner was not yet ready to talk. But this didn't make Jenn's risk any less powerful. She was able to try and, even though she didn't get what she set out to, she was able to channel her desire to process the situation in a way that led to self-reflection and learning. She explained that writing the letter was cathartic and that it helped her name her guilt about moving on in her work. Once she had named that guilt, she was able to face it wholeheartedly.

## Follow the Chocolate Coins

When I try to picture the next right thing to do, what mostly comes to mind are breadcrumbs and chocolate-covered coins. My motto is always this: Let's start with the chocolate. I'm Irish, so St. Patrick's Day is a big deal in our house. When my kids wake me up on the morning of St. Patrick's Day, I roll over and hand them a plastic green cauldron. Their mission is to find and follow a trail of gold candy coins in the house.

The first year we did a hunt for gold coins, my daughter's eyes lit up when she found the first one. But something interesting happened when she found the second. Her brow furrowed and her eyes focused. It's what I've come to know since as her *go mode*. Her brain kicked into gear as if to say, "We're on a mission; let's follow this trail as far as it goes! Also, candy!"

Sometimes it feels as if the Spirit of God works a bit like this—giving us just enough information or direction or motivation to get to the next right step. I wonder if this is how the Samaritan felt that day on the Jericho road. Maybe he couldn't quite see where the road was leading but felt compelled to move step-by-step (or chocolate coin by chocolate coin!) toward wherever that was.

The Samaritan takes risks when he moves toward the man, when he slows down on a dangerous road, when he attaches himself to this traveler for the rest of the trek, when he uses his own resources and then agrees to use more in exchange for the innkeeper looking after the man. Each of these feels like a next doable risk—but nothing about any of these risks feels safe or without real consequence.[2]

A real-person example of someone following the chocolate coins?

To the lawyer seeking an answer about eternal life, Jesus said to treat his neighbor as himself. Take risks in the way you treat people. To the man on a mat seeking healing, Jesus said to take his mat and go. Take a risk by trying to walk in front of all these people.

It's true that sometimes people get the entire vision for their careers all at once. My mom is one of those people. She told me that she knew she wanted to be a counselor when she was a little girl. But I know so many more people who say things such as "If you had told me ten years ago I'd be running this kind of business, I'd have laughed at you" or "I never imagined staying home with my kids, but I love it!" For me, it's been much more like following a path that the Spirit is leading. Each time I take a step, more of the path emerges.

## Be Willing to Face Plant

No matter how small a step or how prudent or sure we might be when we take a risk, sometimes things just don't work out. Sometimes our setbacks feel like little bumps in the road, spots we trip over on our way to wherever we're eventually headed. But other times, we utterly and completely face plant. If not our bodies, surely our hearts bear bruises and scrapes when we fall in this way.

I mentioned earlier that entrepreneurial folks I've studied are much more comfortable talking about failure than they are talking about success. After listening to them, I'm convinced that we can become comfortable with failure when we embrace two truths: (a) setback and pain pave the way for God's liberating love, and (b) failure is an opportunity for learning and growth.

First, embracing risk—and the face planting that sometimes ensues—paves the way for God's liberating love. Of course, God loves us all the time without exception. But when we've taken a risk and it's not gone well, when we're exhausted or beaten down from having face planted, Jesus invites us to draw near:

> Come to me, all you that are weary and are carrying heavy burdens, and I will give you rest. Take my yoke upon you, and learn from me; for I am gentle and humble in heart, and you will find rest for your souls. For my yoke is easy, and my burden is light. (Matt. 11:28–30)

The invitation to draw near to God is a gentle, humble one. It invites us to be humble and gentle in spirit even as we let God pick us up off the pavement.

I've found that embracing God's mercy in the midst of failure is much easier to talk about than to actually live out. That's because I get very, very bootstrappy when I fall. What I mean is that when things seem not to be going well, I just dig in and try harder—probably that good ole Irish Catholic work ethic shining through. Plus, I don't really want anyone to see me face plant. I don't want to have to worry about what folks will think of me or if they'll judge me. It's as if I forget that God's power truly is made perfect in weakness and that God's grace truly is sufficient for our daily, ordinary work.

But God's vision of the good life isn't one in which we spend our resources preserving our self-image. God's vision of the good life isn't one in which individuals are supposed to be heroic or perfect. God's vision of the good life is one of redemption—which comes partly through the promise that God's love never ceases and God's mercy never runs out and that God gifts these to us new each morning (Lam. 3:22–23). This is love—that even when we face plant, there is still a road to walk and a caller who calls.

Dietrich Bonhoeffer, German pastor and author, wrote about resistance and grace in the face of Nazi Germany. His way of explaining grace has been formative for me and I think is helpful for how we might understand God's love when we face plant. Bonhoeffer distinguishes between cheap and costly grace. He writes, "Cheap grace is grace without discipleship, grace without the cross, grace without Jesus Christ, living and incarnate."[3] In contrast, costly grace, well, costs something. Most significantly, love in the form of grace cost the life of Jesus, which beckons us to ongoing and active discipleship that also costs us something.[4] Partly, what discipleship costs us is our willingness to reject any impulse to preserve our self-image and instead to take risks that matter—risks that reveal to the world that we follow God's big story and the Spirit who guides us. Sometimes the results of our risks—whether we're betting the farm or taking the next doable risk—will feel glorious and fruitful. Other times, things won't go as we imagined, and we'll feel like we face planted. Even when we follow the proverbial chocolate coins laid out for us by the Spirit of God, we cannot expect that everything will be neat and tidy. The Jericho road is not tidy; it's messy. Plus, God's mission of redemption is messy and beautiful, usually at the exact same time.

Second, failure is an opportunity for learning and growth. Our willingness to face plant exposes us to the deep, rich, liberating mercy of God, who loves us. And in the process, we learn a whole lot. First comes love, then learning. Learning and growth are at the heart of what it means to be a disciple in the world. Our capacity to learn and grow—and to let God transform our minds along the way—doesn't just happen automatically.[5] We have to be willing to learn and grow and be transformed.

**EXERCISE: A Catalog of Risk**

Journal or reflect on the following questions:

1. Where did you take a risk or notice someone else take a risk today or this week?
2. Does risk-taking come naturally to you? Or do you have to work at it? Do you sense a need to set any boundaries with risk-taking?
3. Where might God be calling you to consider taking the next doable risks?

# Reflect on Where You've Been

In the beginning of this book, I suggested that the way to get where you want to go is to get really honest about where you are—to give yourself over to the internal work of letting what you long for out of its hiding place and into the light. Here, I want to bookend this initial suggestion with another one: *the only way to keep moving forward is to reflect on where you've been.*

Reflection is the intentional practice of pausing to consider what has happened and what it has to teach us. In the midst of a life that is moving rapidly, reflection is part pause and part curiosity. It's taking the time to slow our minds and hearts and bodies so that we can ask, *What happened? What worked? What didn't? What are we learning?* Sometimes reflection happens when we collect feedback and evaluate goals. Other times it happens when we sit quietly at the feet of our experiences and mine what we've learned on the road we've walked so far.

When I teach, I often ask people two questions about their natural relationship with reflection: First, on a scale of 1–10, how *comfortable* are you with reflection? A 1 indicates you are not comfortable doing reflection; 10 means reflection is your favorite thing in the world. Go ahead, answer it for yourself. Second, on a scale of 1–10, how *often* do you spend time reflecting? A 1 indicates you spend very little time reflecting; 10 indicates that reflection is part of your daily rhythm. Again, think about your own number.

Over time, I've noticed that often people's comfort numbers are higher than their frequency numbers. Meaning that for the most part, we like reflection. But that doesn't mean we have the time or space to actually do it. Of course, there are exceptions. Some of us in fact don't like to reflect. For whatever reason, we find it uncomfortable or unhelpful. But for most of us, our biggest obstacle when it comes to reflection is not that we don't like to do it. It's that in an always-on, on-demand culture, it's hard to make intentional space to quiet our racing minds and sit with our experiences so that we can know what it is they have to teach us.

In order to truly make sense of all that's happening in and around us, we need space. Space from the change and the noise and the demands. Space to listen and process and pray. Over time, I have learned that just when I feel I can't afford the space to reflect, that it's a luxury I don't have time for—that is when I have to step back. That is when I have to turn away from whatever I'm doing and run deliberately toward the arms of God. Otherwise, I am bound to repeat the parts of my life that are making me feel so overwhelmed. I am bound to repeat what I have not reflected on and learned from.

## Use the Rhythm of Action, Reflection, Action

In my field of practical theology, we are guided by a rhythm that undergirds nearly everything we research and do. The rhythm is the move from action to reflection and back to action again. Though the movement might sound simple, it's not a given. We don't automatically reflect after we act. And we don't automatically let our reflections guide our future actions. No, we have to intentionally seek this rhythm in our lives and work. A single word for this rhythm might very well be *iteration*.

Paulo Freire is a seminal thinker on education. His work came to me by way of a grad school professor, Mark Lau Branson, and has ever since been foundational for my thinking on how people grow and change. In *Pedagogy of the Oppressed*, Freire writes, "Knowledge emerges only through invention and re-invention, through the restless, impatient, continuing, hopeful inquiry human beings pursue in the world, with the world, and with each other."[1]

In other words, our capacity to grow and change, as you may have realized by now, is central to how we engage in meaningful work in a changing world. It's not so much that we try to change everything around us, but rather we ourselves change. And that engaging with a changing world as a changing person sets us up for the dynamic stability we need to traverse the rapids that are ahead of us.

Now back to Freire. One of the central lessons across Freire's work is that a person's life experience is not only valid but is also a critical source of material from which each of us can learn. In other words, we don't come to classrooms or books or churches or work as blank slates. We come as people full of formative experiences. Unpacking those formative experiences in conversation with new ideas that we engage—well, that's when the best kind of growth and change can happen.

Part of the work of growth requires us to ask reflection questions to ourselves. We must mine our lives for what they are teaching us. The tools we get from experts or friends or even the Bible are always in conversation with our lived experience, never separate. But accessing our own experiences doesn't always feel clear-cut or even possible. It's sometimes hard to know: What actually happened when I took a risk? How do I actually feel about the results? How does what happened inform the way forward? As we try to make our way to these kinds of questions and any answers that follow, it helps to remember that we don't hold all of our knowing in our heads. Whether in our bodies, our emotions, or our visual imaginations, God has wired us with different ways to listen to ourselves.

Jessica Jackley was quick to tell me that the best work she's done has come from two things: using her voice and iteration. On using her voice, Jessica was so clear and convicting that I've carried her words with me as truth since our conversation. Success for Jessica was an outpouring of her being authentic and true to herself. She was sure of her responsibility—to both the world and herself—to speak from the unique perspective only she could have.[2] It makes sense, then, that using her voice in this way meant that she had to come to know her voice. And that coming to know her voice in this way took reflection—listening to her own life and her own words in a quiet space where she could hear her own voice more deeply.

On iteration, the way Jessica described Kiva's iterative life cycle embodied much of the rhythm of *action, reflection, action*. She was quick to admit that not everything has endless opportunities for iteration and refinement—that there are real-life consequences. However, particularly in our work, she described how she's come to learn that "it's going to be just an endless process of learning and getting better and better." She described that kind of iteration as a "beautiful way to live and work."[3]

Kiva's initial round of loan facilitation was $3,000. They weren't able to take money online. It was, in Jessica's words, "scrappy." But by the end of the first year they had iterated their basic idea pretty quickly. Lending was on the rise too. They facilitated $500,000 in loans. The next year it was $50,000,000. In these emails, photos, and overall iteration, we see the movement between action and reflection take place.

In the parable of the good Samaritan, the way Jesus tells the story helps us imagine how the rhythm of action and reflection play out. Jesus told the lawyer that the Samaritan took the hurt man into town and set him up at an inn, paying the innkeeper to look after him. But that's not all the Samaritan did. He went further. The Samaritan told the innkeeper that he was going to return and when he did he would reimburse the innkeeper for any extra expenses he incurred. The Samaritan plans to come back. He intentionally builds in time to come back and ask, What happened?

## After Risk, Reflect by Asking *What Happened?*

What does reflection look like when we consider empathy, imagination, and risk?

A few years back, I felt as if I was drowning in my work because I had said yes to too many things. Saying no has always been hard for me. But there I was on the brink of having my second child, and I was exhausted. I longed for deep, transformative rest before the chaos of life with a newborn.

I thought maybe this process of moving from empathy to imagination to risk to reflection could help me free up the space I so desperately wanted. So I started with practicing empathy along the way. As I thought about the people with whom I was already on the way, especially in my work, there were a handful of folks who stuck out to me as people God might be inviting me to move toward—my husband, some trusted collaborators at Long Winter Media, various clients we served, and my colleagues at the seminary where I work. As I was brainstorming with another woman in the cohort, she encouraged me to move toward some of the people I worked with at the seminary.

Throughout the course of my typical one-on-one meetings with people on my team, I decided to ask one simple question of everyone: What are your hopes for your career over the next year or two? And then I just listened. Based on what I heard from one guy, I started to wonder if I could give him any of my tasks that aligned with his goals. One of the things he had talked about was developing more experience leading meetings. I thought, *What if I had him take over a regular weekly meeting that I run?* That would allow him to have some experience with leading meetings, and it would allow me to convert one of my yeses into a no.

226

We decided together to take the next doable risk to see what happened. The next risk for him was to guest lead an upcoming meeting. After the meeting, he and I made some space to reflect together on how it went: What happened? What worked? What didn't? We both agreed that it had gone pretty well. Then I made some space to reflect on how it went for me: Did it help address my pain point? Move me a bit closer to my longing for rest? Though not all at once, I could imagine how over time it would really help. So he started leading these meetings more often, with us debriefing after each one, until eventually he was the only one to lead them. Later on (and not remembering that I used to lead these meetings!), one of our other colleagues basically went on and on about how much better these meetings were than they used to be. I just smiled. I had one less thing on my plate. My colleague was getting experience that was helping him grow professionally. Plus, our entire team and the mission of our organization was better served by these meetings.

Key to this experiment working out was that we created the intentional space to ask, What happened? It served as a guidepost for us as we moved from action to reflection and back to action again. In this way, we were iterating. Iterating is the result of moving between action and reflection, asking questions such as What happened? and How can we improve? along the way.

## Remember and Give Thanks for What God Has Done

There is a deep relationship between remembrance and gratitude in the Scriptures. Consider God's relationship to the Israelites. In the book of Deuteronomy, after forty years of wandering in the desert, the Israelites are about to enter into the promised land (after some doubt and protest). Before they enter, Moses has a message for the people of Israel. Drawing from Deuteronomy 8, the message in so many words is this: Remember and give thanks for all that God has done. Remember the way that God brought you out of Egypt and then stuck with you and led you through the wilderness. And if you find yourself prospering in the promised land—this land full of olives and figs and honey? Don't get too proud of yourself. Don't think you did all this. Remember God who made water flow from rock and fed you manna in the wilderness when you were thirsty and hungry. In other words, remember that you are a day-by-day, on-the-way people, following a God who indeed guides in the desert and promised land alike.

In this, the Israelites are commissioned to go forward, living and working in a way that reveals they actively remember—and give thanks for—God's leading and protection. The fact that Moses has to remind the Israelites of this reveals a tendency that we see in them and all of humanity—the tendency to forget God when things are going well. But Moses's words help us know that at all times—whether on the brink of failure or success—God desires that we remember all that God has done for us.

Jesus too commissions his disciples to give thanks and remember what God has done. At the Last Supper, Jesus took bread, gave thanks for it, and broke it. Then he gave the bread to his disciples and said, "This is my body given for you; do this in remembrance of me" (Luke 22:19). He repeats this same striking statement about the cup—that it is Christ's blood given for the people. In this, Jesus invites his disciples into an active remembrance that shapes our belonging and our actions. Our commission is to give thanks that Jesus's body and blood are given for us and to remember this in all we do in our lives and work.

What does it look like for us to *remember what God has done* as we put our hands to our everyday work? Andrew Laffoon, founder of the popular photo book company Mixbook, has a practice that helps him remember, focusing especially on gratitude. Andrew drew inspiration from the story of Samuel, who marks the help of God with a physical sign of remembrance—a stone. Samuel names the stone Ebenezer, which quite literally translates as "stone of help" (1 Sam. 7:12).

Andrew starts each workweek with a set of personal reflection questions that help him remember what God has done in his life and work. His practice of remembering starts with what he's thankful for; he especially focuses on what God has done just that previous week. From this, he's able to be honest about his fears and his hopes and where in his life he's dependent on things that don't have anything to do with God. He's able to ask honest questions about whom he needs to forgive and ways he can deepen his trust in God. Each learning lesson—each thing that God has done—becomes like an Ebenezer memorial stone for Andrew.[4]

When I think about the power of Andrew's weekly practice, I'm struck by the rhythm of action and reflection and his focus on what happened through the lens of remembering what God had done. At the close of this chapter, I've included my own version of a memorial-stone practice. For now, consider this: How might you create space to remember what God has done in order to let that remembrance and gratitude actively shape your way forward?

## Remember That We're an On-the-Way People

Many of the models of how to do work and life and how to start things don't necessarily mirror the patterns of redemption we see in the Bible. From hustle culture to the narrative that we ought to be the center of our goals, there's so much out there that feels contradictory to the work of God and our commission to belong to Jesus and be an on-the-way people.

My friend Bethany is especially tuned in to this dynamic. One day, we were walking back to the campus where we both worked. The sun was bright, and we were both looking down at the pavement when the crosswalk sign started beeping. Engrossed in conversation, we looked up and stepped out to cross the road. Bethany was in the thick of starting a church, needing to process all that comes with birthing a living, breathing organization into the world. I was acting as a sounding board for her ideas. She had asked me for help with strategy and marketing. I was energized about her work and how God was so obviously working through her.

I was throwing out a bunch of ideas about how she could tend to the needs of her budding congregation. I was mid-monologue when I noticed her eyes drift back down to the pavement (and this time not because of the sun). She shifted just a bit in her stride, turned to me, and asked, "Do I really have to do it that way? The uninspired, formulaic way everyone else starts things? The endless self-promotion? The endless hustle? Surely there's another way."

I couldn't believe how antithetical my ideas for her were to all that I've written about in this book. I gave her no ideas for trusting creativity, empathizing, or taking small, doable risks. I gave no encouragement to consider the manna that God delivers each morning amid a larger world of chaos and disruption. Instead of leaning in and letting go, I was telling her to power up and press go!

In her gentle and wise pushback, I was reminded yet again that there is such deep comfort in the truth that—guided by a God who loves us—we are indeed an on-the-way people. The fruits of redemption do not bloom overnight. We cannot muscle our way to resurrection. We cannot go forward without first moving toward others and having compassion for ourselves. I was reminded that seizing opportunity and creating value don't look the same for all people or even sometimes from one day to the next. I was reminded that the next doable risk is just one step and that the ground may indeed shift beneath us tomorrow.

I was reminded that so much of the meaningful work we crave is found when we embrace our own growth as followers of Jesus. When our work is less about changing the entire world and more about being a people who grow and change, alongside others, for the sake of God's redemptive work in the world.

## Commission for Your Road Ahead

In the first chapter of this book, I listed a host of reasons that might have brought you to this book. Among these were that maybe you've wanted to change careers, or you need help integrating all your ideas. Maybe you feel overwhelmed by change, or you are craving deeper meaning in your work.

Whatever brought you to this book and whatever resonated in these pages, I want to send you off with a benediction for the way forward. This is my prayer for you and for myself and for anyone who seeks meaningful work and the way of Jesus in a changing world.

Whether you're at the start of something new or wondering what comes next—*may you take care and take heart on this wild and wonderful road.*

For the days when your work feels boring or meaningless—*may you smell and taste the grace of God that comes by way of manna each new morning. And in that, may you trust that because God is near and you belong to God, your work cannot be without meaning.*

For the days when it feels like the ground shifts beneath you—*may you feel held by the Lord who is a very present help in times of trouble. May this enable you to lean in and let go even as it feels as though the world is turning upside down.*

For the days when change feels utterly disorienting, when you feel like you're riding down Class IV rapids without a paddle—*may you trust that God who created the current in the sea guides your boat as well.*

For the days when you feel hope burst in like a bright and beautiful song—*may you let the joy of this life and the labor that's woven into it completely wash over you.*

For the days when your longings make their way from hidden places in your heart and out into the light—*may you know that God celebrates your bravery.*

For the days when you feel that you don't have it in you to move toward others—*may you remember that sometimes loving your neighbor and yourself look completely different than you've been told.*

For the days when the choices in front of you feel scary—*may you take heart that Jesus called his disciples off the shores to walk step-by-step behind him. And Jesus will guide you, like he did them, as you take your next doable risk.*

For the days when you face plant, when all that you've hoped for feels far off and you're left with nothing but shame—*may you know that resilience is a gift of resurrection. And that because death never has the final word, your failures will never define you.*

For the days when you feel most in sync with God's mission of redemption—*may you look to the left and to the right and thank God for the relationships that root you.*

For the days when you take a step toward others or toward yourself or even toward the big ideas that beckon you—*may you feel God's warm smile and tender touch and remember that you and I and all of us are indeed meaningful parts of God's creation.*

*Blessings on your road ahead.*

## EXERCISE: Create Memorial Stones

What follows is inspired by Andrew Laffoon's practice but with my own modifications to help you apply the themes of this chapter. To create your own memorial stone practice, take the following steps:

1. Commit the same hour of your week to this practice for at least six weeks.

2. Decide up front the questions you want to ask yourself. Sample questions include:

   a. What did I learn last week?

   b. Where was God in that learning?

   c. When was I afraid or insecure this week?

   d. What parts of that fear or insecurity do I need to invite God into?

   e. Who do I need to forgive this week?

   f. How did God surprise me this past week?

   g. What do I find myself hoping God will do this coming week?

3. Record your answers in a journal.

4. Decide on an icon that will represent your Ebenezer stone—maybe it's a flower from your garden or an animal you love. Maybe it's a Bible verse you find or a literal rock from outside. As you journal and name what God has done, draw or tape an image of your icon next to each lesson you want to capture. You may also want to place physical reminders on your desk or in your office.

5. After you've done this for several weeks, notice the patterns that arise as you trace back through your icons in your journal.

# *Notes*

## Chapter 1  Name Where You're Stuck

1. Walter Brueggemann, *Genesis* (Louisville: John Knox, 1982), 260–72.

2. Diane Mulcahy, *The Gig Economy: The Complete Field Guide to Getting Better Work, Taking More Time Off, and Financing the Life You Want* (New York: Amazon, 2017), 2.

3. Marion McGovern, *Thriving in the Gig Economy: How to Capitalize and Compete in the New World of Work* (Wayne, NJ: Career Press, 2017), 28; MBO Partners, *America's Independents: A Rising Economic Force*, 2016, 3, https://www.mbopartners.com/wp-content/uploads /2019/02/2016_MBO_Partners_State_of_Independence_Report.pdf.

4. Emily Nagoski and Amelia Nagoski, *Burnout: The Secret to Unlocking the Stress Cycle* (New York: Ballantine Books, 2019); Anne Helen Peterson, *Can't Even: How Millennials Became the Burnout Generation* (New York: Houghton Mifflin Harcourt, 2020).

5. The work of psychologist Alice Boyles has been helpful for me here. See Alice Boyles, *The Anxiety Toolkit: Strategies for Fine-Tuning Your Mind and Moving Past Your Stuck Points* (New York: Penguin Random House, 2015).

## Chapter 2  Lean In and Let Go

1. Reid Hoffman and Ben Casnocha, *The Start-Up of You: Adapt to the Future, Invest in Yourself, and Transform Your Career* (New York: Crown, 2012), 5.

2. Thomas Friedman, *Thank You for Being Late: An Optimist's Guide to Thriving in the Age of Accelerations* (New York: Farrar, Straus & Giroux), 198–99.

3. Ronald A. Heifetz and Marty Linsky, *Leadership on the Line: Staying Alive through the Dangers of Leading* (Boston: Harvard Business School Press, 2002); see also Ronald A. Heifetz and Donald L. Laurie, "The Work of Leadership," *Harvard Business Review* (1997): 124–27.

4. Heifetz and Linsky, *Leadership on the Line*; see also Heifetz and Laurie, "Work of Leadership."

5. I learned the phrase *cultivating instincts* from Scott Cormode, which he explains in *Making Spiritual Sense: Christian Leaders as Spiritual Interpreters* (Nashville: Abingdon, 2006). He expands the idea in order to help churches innovate in *The Innovative Church: How Leaders and Their Congregations Can Adapt in an Ever-Changing World* (Grand Rapids: Baker Academic, 2020).

## Chapter 3  Believe That You Are Called

1. Bryant Myers, *Engaging Globalization: The Poor, Christian Mission, and Our Hyper Connected World* (Grand Rapids: Baker Academic, 2017), 102.

2. In 2018, I cowrote a four-part series entitled Myths of Vocation with Jerome Blanco and Paul Matsushima, two colleagues from Fuller's De Pree Center. Our four parts took up four dysfunctional beliefs about calling: *If I Check All the Boxes, I'll Be Fulfilled*; *My Calling Is My Job*; *I'm Called to One Special Thing*; and *It All Happens Right Away*. Though this section on dealing with dysfunction is distinct, it is influenced by this project and these colleagues and the stories we captured along the way. Myths of Vocation can be downloaded for free at https://depree.org/workbooks/myths/.

3. Juliana Menasce Horowitz and Nikki Graf, "Most U.S. Teens See Anxiety and Depression as a Major Problem among Their Peers," Pew Research Center, February 20, 2019, https://www.pewsocialtrends.org/2019/02/20/most-u-s-teens-see-anxiety-and-depression-as-a-major-problem-among-their-peers/.

4. The work of Tod Bolsinger has been helpful in my own search to name why we can't treat God's callings like something just waiting to be found. See Tod Bolsinger, "Formed, Not Found," Fuller Studio, accessed March 15, 2021, https://fullerstudio.fuller.edu/formed-not-found/.

5. Derek Thompson, "Workism Is Making Americans Miserable," *Atlantic*, February 24, 2019, https://www.theatlantic.com/ideas/archive/2019/02/religion-workism-making-americans-miserable/583441/.

6. William Placher, *Callings: Twenty Centuries of Christian Wisdom on Vocation* (Grand Rapids: Eerdmans, 2005), 6.

7. Placher, *Callings*, 6; Lee Hardy, *The Fabric of This World: Inquiries into Calling, Career Choice, and the Design of Human Work* (Grand Rapids: Eerdmans, 1990), 45.

8. Hardy, *Fabric of This World*, 45.

9. Rom. 5:1.

10. Puritans later referred to these as a general calling and a particular calling; see Placher, *Callings*, 206.

11. Rom. 1:6; 1 Cor. 1:2.

12. Matt. 4:18–20; Luke 5:27–28.

## Chapter 4  Walk the Entrepreneurial Way

1. I originally surveyed forty-seven entrepreneurs. In a follow-up, I surveyed six more. See Michaela O'Donnell Long, "Adopting an Entrepreneurial Posture: Vocational Formation for a Changing World of Work" (PhD diss., Fuller Seminary, 2018), 164–214. After the formal research project, I posed these same questions to hundreds of people in workshops and classes and observed the patterns of their responses.

2. Amy Sherman, "Introduction," *Kingdom Calling: Vocational Stewardship for the Common Good* (Downers Grove, IL: InterVarsity, 2011), Kindle loc. 95. Sherman draws on Timothy J. Keller, "Creation Care and Justice," sermon delivered at Redeemer Presbyterian Church, New York, January 16, 2005.

3. Sherman, "What Does a Rejoiced City Look Like?, "*Kingdom Calling*, Kindle loc. 211.

4. Perry Yoder, *Shalom: The Bible's Word for Salvation, Justice, and Peace* (Eugene, OR: Wipf & Stock, 2017). Yoder argues that Psalm 10 demonstrates that evil people are the ones who are against the poor. The psalm includes a plea for God's justice as God is the source of justice for the weak. See page 30.

5. Sherman, "What Does a Rejoiced City Look Like?," Kindle loc. 200.

6. Sherman, "What Does a Rejoiced City Look Like?," Kindle loc. 218.

7. Sherman, "What Does a Rejoiced City Look Like?," Kindle loc. 246.

8. Sherman, "What Does a Rejoiced City Look Like?," Kindle loc. 246.

9. Yoder explains that there are three meanings for *shalom* in the Old Testament: "First, it can refer to a material and physical state of affairs, this being its most frequent usage. It can also refer to relationships, and here it comes closest in meaning to the English word *peace*. And finally it also has a moral sense, which is its least frequent meaning." On the first usage, see Gen. 29:6; 37:14; Exod. 18:7; 1 Sam. 17:18; 2 Sam. 11:7; 18:29; 2 Kings 4:26; and Esther 2:11. On the second usage, see Gen. 26:29,

31; Josh. 9:15; Judg. 4:17; and 1 Kings 5:12. On the third usage, see 2 Kings 5:19; Pss. 34:14; and 37:37. See Yoder, *Shalom*, 10–16.

10. Sherman, *Kingdom Calling*, Kindle loc. 283.

11. Sherman, *Kingdom Calling*, Kindle loc. 283–332. Sherman's usage of *peace* here is consistent with Yoder's second definition of *shalom* in the Old Testament, *shalom* as relational justice. See Yoder, *Shalom*, 13.

12. Ruth Haley Barton, *Strengthening the Soul of Your Leadership: Seeking God in the Crucible of Ministry* (Downers Grove, IL: InterVarsity Press, 2012), 47.

13. Peace with others can also include security around a lack of violence (Ps. 46:9; Mic. 4:3; Ezek. 34:27–28). See Sherman, *Kingdom Calling*, Kindle loc. 342–60.

14. Sherman, *Kingdom Calling*, Kindle loc. 370–89.

15. Sherman, *Kingdom Calling*, Kindle loc. 378. Tom Nelson writes about the interplay of human and economic flourishing. He argues that "we must grasp with both our mind and our heart that human flourishing and economic flourishing go hand in hand. Good neighbors make good neighborhoods, and good neighborhoods make good neighbors." See Tom Nelson, *The Economics of Neighborly Love: Investing in Your Community's Compassion and Capacity* (Downers Grove, IL: InterVarsity, 2017), 70–71.

16. Tom Kelley and David Kelley, *Creative Confidence: Unleashing the Creative Potential within Us All* (New York: Crown, 2013), 2–5.

17. Tom Kelley and David Kelley, "Reclaim Your Creative Confidence," *Harvard Business Review* (December 2012): 2.

18. Brené Brown, *Daring Greatly: How the Courage to Be Vulnerable Transforms the Way We Live, Love, Parent, and Lead* (New York: Avery, 2012), 58.

19. Brené Brown, "Shame and Vulnerability," Work of the People, accessed January 20, 2018, http://www.theworkofthepeople.com/shame -and-vulnerability.

## Chapter 5 Be Rooted in Relationships

1. Andrew Laffoon, telephone interview with the author, April 12, 2017.

2. Laffoon, interview.

3. Laffoon, interview.

4. Laffoon, interview.

5. Uli Chi, telephone interview with the author, April 26, 2017.

6. Alex Lim, Zoom interview with the author, April 24, 2017.

7. Andy Crouch, *Culture Making: Recovering Our Creative Calling* (Downers Grove, IL: InterVarsity, 2013), 239.

8. Crouch, *Culture Making*, 240. Crouch suggests three as the optimal number for this group, although four or five may also be desirable.

9. Crouch, *Culture Making*, 105.

10. Ed Catmull with Amy Wallace, *Creativity, Inc.: Overcoming the Unseen Forces That Stand in the Way of True Inspiration* (New York: Random House, 2014), 86–87.

11. Catmull with Wallace, *Creativity, Inc.*, 90.

### Chapter 6 Trust Your Creativity

1. Sarah Contrucci Smith, telephone interview with the author, April 5, 2017.

2. Crouch, *Culture Making*, 104.

3. Contrucci Smith, interview.

4. Contrucci Smith, interview.

5. Jürgen Moltmann, *God in Creation: A New Theology of Creation and the Spirit of God* (Minneapolis: Fortress, 1993), 54.

6. Moltmann, *God in Creation*, 54.

7. Steven M. Smith et al., "Empirical Studies of Creative Cognition in Idea Generation," in *Creativity and Innovation in Organizational Teams*, ed. Leigh L. Thompson and Hoon Seok Choi (Mahwah, NJ: Lawrence Erlbaum Associates, 2006), 4.

8. Smith et al., "Empirical Studies," 9; Teresa M. Amabile and Mukti Khaire, "Creativity and the Role of the Leader," *Harvard Business Review* (October 2008): 104.

9. Crouch, *Culture Making*, 104.

10. Wayne Muller, *Sabbath: Finding Rest, Renewal, and Delight in Our Busy Lives* (New York: Bantam Books, 1999), 1.

### Chapter 7 Build Resilience

1. The Knight Foundation and the Solo City Project, "Solo City Report: A New World of Work Is Here, and We Are Not Ready," 2016, 97.

2. Mindy Bostick, "Building Resilience from Disruption," *Harvard Business Review* (September 28, 2017): 1. According to this report, resiliency is "a set of personal skills and processes that enable individuals at all levels to reduce stress but perform well under it, learn continuously, and keep their work and life responsibilities in harmony."

3. See Detroit Soup, https://detroitsoup.com.

4. Amy Kaherl, phone interview with the author, April 3, 2017.

5. Kaherl, interview.

6. Kaherl, interview.

7. Kaherl, interview.

8. See Yellow Co., http://yellowco.co.

9. Joanna Waterfall, telephone interview with the author, April 18, 2017.

10. Richard Rohr, "Transforming Pain," Center for Action and Contemplation, October 17, 2018, emphasis original, https://cac.org/transforming-pain-2018-10-17/.

## Chapter 8  Practice Empathy along the Way

1. "Daniel Goleman on the Three Kinds of Empathy," *Super Soul Sunday*, Oprah Winfrey Network, March 20, 2016, http://www.oprah.com/own-super-soul-sunday/daniel-goleman-on-the-three-kinds-of-empathy-video. See also Daniel Goleman, Richard Boyatzis, and Annie McKee, *Primal Leadership: Learning to Lead with Emotional Intelligence* (Boston: Harvard Business School Press, 2004).

2. "About Kiva," Kiva, accessed August 2, 2020, https://www.kiva.org/about.

3. Jessica Jackley, telephone interview with the author, April 19, 2017.

4. Jackley, interview.

5. Rohr, "Transforming Pain," emphasis original.

## Chapter 9  Convert Empathy into Imagination

1. Rachel Goble, telephone interview with the author, April 5, 2017.

2. Goble, interview.

3. Jackley, interview.

4. Margaret R. Somers, "The Narrative Construction of Identity: A Relational and Network Approach," *Theory and Society* 23 (1994): 613–14.

## Chapter 10  Take the Next Doable Risks

1. Bill Burnett and Dave Evans, *Designing Your Life: How to Build a Well-Lived, Joyful Life* (New York: Knopf, 2016), 118.

2. In his commentary on the Gospel of Luke, Joel Green writes this of the Samaritan: "He stops on the Jericho road to assist someone he does not know in spite of the self-evident peril of doing so; he gives of his own goods and money, freely, making no arrangements for reciprocation; in order to obtain care for this stranger, he enters an inn, itself a place of potential danger, and he even enters into an open-ended monetary relationship with the innkeeper, a relationship in which the chance of extortion is high." See Joel B. Green, *The Gospel of Luke*, in The New International Commentary on the New Testament (Grand Rapids: Eerdmans, 1997), 432.

3. Dietrich Bonhoeffer, *The Cost of Discipleship* (New York: Touchstone, 1959), 45.

4. Bonhoeffer, *Cost of Discipleship*, 45.

5. Jennifer Woodruff Tait, "A Living Sacrifice," Fuller De Pree Center, August 23, 2020, https://depree.org/a-living-sacrifice/.

## Chapter 11  Reflect on Where You've Been

1. Paulo Freire, *Pedagogy of the Oppressed: 50th Anniversary Edition* (New York: Bloomsbury Academic, 2012), 72.

2. Jackley, interview.

3. Jackley, interview.

4. Laffoon, interview.

# *Acknowledgments*

Thank you to the team at Baker Books—your warm welcome and sound wisdom helped me to find my footing in an unfamiliar world. Eileen Hanson, Wendy Wetzel, Laura Palma, Brian Thomasson, Barb Barnes, Giséle Mix, and everyone else—you're not only a world-class team, you're wonderful humans. Stephanie Smith, you've elevated my writing and helped me to know new things about myself. It's such a gift that life's twists and turns have enabled our shared work.

Greg Johnson, you have been exactly what I needed in this process. I am grateful for your kindness and guidance at every turn.

Thank you to the folks who were willing to talk as part of my original dissertation research project: Uli Chi, Jessica Jackley, Joanna Waterfall, Sarah Contrucci Smith, Amy Kaherl, Alex Lim, Andrew Laffoon, Rachel Goble, and others, your stories are generous and instructive.

To those who have believed in me and this book, in some cases before I could see it myself, thank you. Scott Cormode, Mark Lau Branson, Tod Bolsinger, Kara Powell, Jody Vanderwel, and Uli Chi, from opening doors to counseling me on which ones to walk through, I deeply appreciate your wisdom and feedback at every turn.

Mark Roberts, thank you for encouraging me to write this book and for constantly championing it (and me) to anyone who would listen. I am grateful to you and the entire De Pree Center team for your encouragement in this process.

To the friends who made space in conversation for this book or read early drafts, your wisdom and love shaped the contours of this project more than you may know. Angela Williams Gorrell, Elizabeth McQuitty, Kathy Young, and Tracy Matthews, you helped the ideas in the book get clear and relatable, and for that I am grateful. Lyndsey Deane Ratchford, Beth McQuitty, Amy Richard, and Brandon Richard, your friendship buoyed me when I needed it.

Dad and Cathy, Mom and Mark, Jim, and Bonnie, thank you for the constant encouragement. Mom and Dad, not everyone grows up with parents who are both entrepreneurs. From the early days, you shaped my imagination about both what was possible and what work that mattered looked like.

Mom, you read so many early drafts of this book. And each time you reveled in them in the way only you can do. Thank you.

My heart swells every time I think of how I wrote the pages of this book while holding Sage or watching Evelyn run around the yard. Kids, your presence is inextricably woven into these pages, and for that I am grateful. And to Dan. You did way more than your fair share around the house and with the kids so that I could write this book. Plus, you were the one who helped me workshop every early idea on these pages, often offering me theological insight that helped unlock what felt stuck. I am thankful that this book is part of our life, love, and shared work. I love you.

Thanks to God, who has already said that every one of us matters and that the work of our hands and our hearts matters too.

**Michaela O'Donnell,** PhD, is executive director of Fuller Seminary's De Pree Center for Leadership. She is an entrepreneur, a teacher, and a sought-after speaker and consultant who regularly presents on the topics of vocation, career, and leadership to religious, secular, academic, and lay audiences.

# CONNECT WITH MICHAELA AND THE DE PREE CENTER

To find out more about Michaela's work and research, you can visit her on social media at

| | |
|---|---|
| michaela.odonnell | depreecenter |
| depreecenter | DePreeCenter |

# WANT MORE DISCERNMENT TOOLS?

Here at the Max De Pree Center for Leadership, we provide leaders like you with experiences that help you grow in your sense of purpose, deal with issues that matter, and move toward greater fruitfulness in whatever work God has called you to do. From our cohorts who help you discern God's callings to a daily devotional for leaders, we've spent years turning research into resources, with the goal of helping people like you respond faithfully to God in all seasons of your life and leadership.

## Equipping

Marketplace Leaders – Young Professionals – Retired Leaders

## Depree.org